→SAGE

Get a Better Grade

Seven Steps to Excellent Essays and Assignments

Mal Leicester & Denise Taylor

 **$SAGE**

Los Angeles | London | New Delhi
Singapore | Washington DC | Melbourne

Los Angeles | London | New Delhi
Singapore | Washington DC | Melbourne

SAGE Publications Ltd
1 Oliver's Yard
55 City Road
London EC1Y 1SP

SAGE Publications Inc.
2455 Teller Road
Thousand Oaks, California 91320

SAGE Publications India Pvt Ltd
B 1/I 1 Mohan Cooperative Industrial Area
Mathura Road
New Delhi 110 044

SAGE Publications Asia-Pacific Pte Ltd
3 Church Street
#10-04 Samsung Hub
Singapore 049483

Editor: Jai Seaman
Assistant editor: Alysha Owen
Production editor: Katherine Haw
Copyeditor: Catja Pafort
Proofreader: Rebecca Storr
Indexer: Elizabeth Ball
Marketing manager: Catherine Slinn
Cover design: Shaun Mercier
Typeset by: C&M Digitals (P) Ltd, Chennai, India
Printed in the UK

© Mal Leicester and Denise Taylor 2017

First published 2017

Library of Congress Control Number: 2017933881

British Library Cataloguing in Publication data

A catalogue record for this book is available from the British Library

ISBN 978-1-4739-4897-6
ISBN 978-1-4739-4898-3 (pbk)

At SAGE we take sustainability seriously. Most of our products are printed in the UK using FSC papers and boards. When we print overseas we ensure sustainable papers are used as measured by the PREPS grading system. We undertake an annual audit to monitor our sustainability.

Summary of Contents

Contents

About the Authors

Professor Mal Leicester is Emeritus Professor at the University of Nottingham where she held the chair of adult learning and teaching. She was responsible for monitoring departmental assessments (criteria and consistency). She marked assignments at all levels both as an internal and an external Examiner and for the work of graduate and postgraduate students and supervised student dissertations and theses in philosophy, multicultural education, moral education, ethical issues and inclusive education.

Previously Mal was senior lecturer in continuing education at the University of Warwick. She has been a secondary school teacher, was the county of Avon's advisor for multicultural education and the director of a community organisation in Birmingham.

Mal has written a variety of educational books and papers including, most recently, *Can I Tell You about Tourette Syndrome? (A Guide for Friends, Family and Professionals)*.

Dr Denise Taylor is an environmental and wildlife conservation professional with a focus on large carnivores, and in particular wild canids. She was awarded her PhD as a mature student in 2012 in the field of environmental education from the University of Nottingham. Denise has written books and papers on environmental education and canid conservation, and more recently has been involved in education projects on badger conservation in the UK.

As an entrepreneur, Denise is the owner and managing director of Bridge PR & Media Services Limited, where she also delivers educational workshops on marketing strategy, and writing content for press and marketing.

Acknowledgements

We are grateful to Roger Twelvetrees and Cathy McNulty for their encouragement and their advice about and material on engineering and occupational therapy respectively. We would also like to thank Nicola Leicester for material on the topics of nursing and criminality.

We would like to thank Charlotte Taylor for her insights into her studies as an A-Level student and for her patience during the writing process.

Most of all, we are grateful to Jai Seaman, our editor, for her constant support and constructive advice throughout. And also to Katherine Haw for going that extra mile in her production duties.

Introduction

Who Is the Book For?

This book was written for a wide intended readership because all Higher Education (HE) students, undergraduate and postgraduate, and even students doing A-levels want to know how to write a good essay and wish to achieve a high grade. Whether you are a student of education, the arts, of one of the humanities or one of the social sciences you will need to write essays, reports and reviews.

Each chapter contains good advice, explanations and examples, and you will be a much more competent and skilful student after reading it. However, if you are desperately short of time, but need to produce an acceptable essay or assignment, then **at least read the summary at the end of each chapter and at the end of this introduction.** These will give you the most helpful tips, and the most crucial advice to enable you to write a much better essay than you might otherwise have submitted. Similarly, skip to Chapter 1 if you are impatient to read the main book, and return to the introduction at the end.

This book will help you:

- To write your first essay or assignment. This might be your first essay ever or your first essay in a new subject.
- To improve your grades on subsequent essays and assignments.
- If this is the first time you will be assessed for something other than an essay – such as a report, a review or a group presentation.
- If you do not understand what is going wrong. What does your tutor mean by *incorrect referencing, lacks structure, too descriptive,* etc.?
- If you are a student who experiences anxiety about your assignments, especially if there has been a gap in studying. You may worry about producing longer essays at a higher level. It is very common for returning students, who are highly motivated and conscientious, to feel anxious about striving for HE level work. This book will help you.
- If you are a mature student, or indeed a young student coming via an Access or some other less conventional route, you will also benefit from having your own copy. If you are a highly motivated and conscientious student, you will find this book reassuring.
- If you are a **staff member** who is new to marking at this level and who is anxious to grade work fairly and in tune with the assessments of your colleagues. Even some experienced members of staff are secretly puzzled when other colleagues give a lower grade than they have themselves, with comments such as: *insufficiently critical* or, *too assertive.*

How Will This Book Help You to Produce Good Work?

- You will learn how to write a good essay or assignment – an essay which demonstrates the characteristics an assessor will be looking for.
- You will come to understand frequent sources of errors and learn how to avoid the most common pitfalls.
- You will develop the criticality appropriate to Higher Education.

If you are a university or college student, you need to understand what makes for good work in Higher Education. (In Chapter 3, we will explore what working at a *higher* level means.) This concise and practical book will help you to produce competent work at an appropriate level so that you complete your studies successfully.

Two basic requirements of good work are: firstly, to know your subject area, and, secondly, to know how to present what you know in well-written, well-referenced and original work. In conjunction with your subject-specific guidebooks and materials, this book will provide all the support you need.

Every chapter gives examples of right and wrong approaches so that you will know how to work on the right lines. We will also show you how a barely passing level assignment can move, with relatively little additional work, to a good grade. Academic work has established rules and conventions that you are not born knowing. Tutors can sometimes assume that these requirements are obvious and do not need pointing out. On the contrary, you need to learn the rules of the academic game and the chapters in this book will explain, quite explicitly, what these are. An appendix will also show you how to evaluate what you have produced.

Chapters 1, 2 and 7 provide you with the tools to avoid the most basic pitfalls, and thus to produce an acceptable essay or assignment which will not fail. Chapters 3–5 will take you further, equipping you with the critical skills to achieve a higher grade.

The contents of the chapters cover:

- use of the literature and relevant research, planning and organisation
- correct use of reasons and evidence
- critical thinking (including criticality)
- meta-analysis
- developing a fresh point of view
- presentation and referencing.

The 'presentation' chapter looks at the good presentation of written work and also at the correct use of academic conventions such as referencing, acronyms and the avoidance of unintentional plagiarism.

The majority of assignments in HE still come in the form of an essay, but there are other common forms of assignments. These assignments (reports, reviews, presentations, etc.) need to pay attention to all the points made in the preceding chapters (Chapters 1–7), but additionally have a number of particular requirements that you need to understand and fulfil. These other forms of assignment are looked at in Chapters 8 and 9.

Before all these chapters, however, we provide a useful seven-step progress plan below. This will help you to meet your deadlines and word limits. Finally, this introduction explains the seven most common essay and assignment errors, linking these to the chapters.

In short, if you are anxious about your essays and assignments and about how to work at HE level, this book, with its concise explanations, useful checklists and crucial tips, is a must-have book for you. It will also be useful to you if you simply want to get a better grade.

Assignment Anxiety. Getting Started: Writer's Block

Many students, when faced with their first essay, do not know how to get started. They are unsure of what is expected and feel that they may fail to work at the expected level. Other students, having been disappointed by their grade(s) for previous assignments, also lack confidence. They worry about what went wrong. If you have **assignment anxiety** you are not alone. Such anxiety is widespread. It undermines confidence, which may then be reflected in the tentative, unsure tone of your essays. It can even lead to a severe case of writer's block.

Sometimes writer's block causes students to continue their background reading rather indiscriminately. They feel they must read everything. They make copious notes and feel overwhelmed by the sheer mass and complexity of this material. Where should they begin? What should they include and what should they omit? This becomes a vicious circle. The more you put off beginning the writing process, the more overwhelmed and unable to begin you will feel.

There is much advice about overcoming writer's block. These are the five tips which we think are most useful.

1. **You are capable.** Remind yourself that you would not be on the course if your tutors thought that you were not capable of completing it successfully.
2. **Take bite-sized pieces.** Do not sit down intending to write the whole assignment. Following your plan (see Chapter 2), aim to write just one section (or even the first paragraph of the first section). You have begun.
3. **Allow a limited time to complete the section.** For example, do not sit down after breakfast and intend to write for the whole day. Decide you will write for, say, one hour in the morning and for one hour later in the day. (Obviously if you are on a roll, you can continue, but the trick is to aim for small steps, which feel less daunting.)
4. **First draft.** Remember that this is only your first draft. You will be able to improve it; to delete, prune, expand, take advice. It is always easier to work on and improve a first draft than it is to take that first step of putting pen to paper on the icy page.
5. **Seven steps.** Construct a timescale for the seven points of the plan (below) and keep to the time you have allotted for each step.

Seven Steps to Completion

These seven steps will help you to meet your assignment deadline. Divide the time that you have available from now up to your deadline into three equal amounts. You should try to complete steps one and two by the end of the first block of time, steps three and four by the end of the second block and steps five, six and seven by your deadline (see Figure 2.1 on page 29 for a Gantt chart on planning your Seven Steps. A Gantt chart is a tool that is commonly used to manage projects, tasks and events displayed against a timeline and showing the duration of each item or task). These timings are approximate, but should give you a rough guide to keeping you on target.

The Seven Steps

1. Focus and Preparation

The Title. Focus on the essay title. What is it asking? It could be a question. For example: *Environmental Education should be included in the Primary Curriculum. Do you agree?*

You will consider arguments for and against and give your own view with reasons. Your introduction might explore what we mean by environmental education and why it is important. In the main body of the essay you will consider arguments for and against the inclusion of environmental education and give your own view with reasons. Finally your conclusion might touch briefly [because it is not strictly part of the question] on some pedagogical considerations, and summarise the most important arguments for your own point of you.

How many parts does the title have? Students often miss out a part of a two or three-parted title, e.g. *Explain and Evaluate the Arguments for Environmental Education.* You must remember to explain **and** to discuss/evaluate **and**, indeed, to give your own views with reasons.

You could record your initial thoughts about environmental education before you begin your reading, e.g. education must be worthwhile. Is conserving and protecting our environment worthwhile? How? How worthwhile is it relative to other worthwhile learning? i.e. there may not be enough time to include all subjects that could be regarded as worthwhile. You could make a strong argument about how crucial environmental education is for the survival of the planet. Could/should environmental education be taught as a separate curriculum subject or permeate all subjects?

The following essay question has two parts and incorporates two elements in the first part. All this must be taken into account.

Example Title: Explain and discuss Brookfield's Notion of Critical Thinking. Do you consider this to be an influential idea?

Clearly there are three parts to this essay. You must identify and explain each of the components of Brookfield's idea. You must discuss each of these components. And, finally, you must evaluate its influence. For example, it may have been influential in one sector of education or the social sciences and not in others (an example of a poor, and an example of a good attempt at a similar essay are provided in Chapter 4).

Or

Example Title: Explain and discuss Darwin's Theory of Evolution.

This title has two parts. In *explaining* Darwin's theory, you will articulate as clearly as possible the claims of the theory. In *discussing* the theory, you may be identifying its strengths, weaknesses, implications, historical context, influences and subsequent scientific evidential support, etc.

However excellently you write on one part of an essay question, you cannot get a good grade if you neglect another part. A surprisingly large number of students make this basic error, writing much on one part of an essay question and neglecting, completely or relatively, another part or parts. To ensure you answer all parts of a question, list a small number of key points relating to each of the parts of the question. Note a small number of key texts, which are directly relevant to each part.

2. The Literature Search

Now do some directly relevant reading. Obviously include books from your reading list and any relevant books or papers written or recommended by your tutor. There will be more about how to research and record the relevant literature in Chapter 1. You will learn that there are useful tools to help you with this. For example, using digital resources such as Google and other search engines; making good use of your college or university online resources as well as the libraries' physical resources for researching; and taking advantage of the plethora of software packages and programs for capturing and recording the information you found. Using citation management tools and applications is a good starting point for keeping a track of the journals, books and other sources you may discover as you carry out your literature search. These will help you to store and manage the information. You can also use a simple Microsoft Excel spreadsheet or free tools such as Scrivener, Evernote (www.evernote.com) or Trello (www.trello.com). These are also available as apps, making it easier to capture information easily when you are out and about.

3. Planning

Plan your essay. To see the intended structure clearly, it is helpful if this is shown on one side of A4. Chapter 2 gives guidance on how to construct this plan. A good plan will focus on the title and incorporate all its parts in a logical sequence. Planning is essential for good organisation of your material and will also help you to break your writer's block and get started. It will also help you to time plan your writing in order to meet the submission date. Do not launch into your essay without making a plan. Poor organisation of material, including illogical ordering, repetition, serious omissions and jumbled ideas result from lack of initial thinking and planning. A good written plan will help you to produce well-organised work.

4. First Draft

Find somewhere comfortable to write, and, if you can, find somewhere where you do not have too many interruptions or distractions. Remind yourself that this is only your first draft. Nothing is set in stone. However, it is always easier to improve a first draft than to try and produce a perfect piece of work straight off.

Write your first draft following your plan. This will not necessarily mean that you must write in the sequence of the plan; you may want to write the main body before writing the introduction for example. The sequence may vary from essay to essay and from student to student. But you must finish up with an introduction, a main body and a conclusion as set out in your plan. Following your plan will also help you to stay relevant to your essay title. Superfluous material, however excellent, will nevertheless be marked down if it is not relevant to the question asked. Check that you have answered the question as given, e.g. 'give three reasons' means three. If you only give two reasons, you will lose marks and giving four will not mean you will gain additional marks.

5. Second Draft

Now read your completed essay and, using the checklists provided at the end of the book, you can add, change, amend and delete. Add these notes to (a copy of) the text of your first draft. Some of the most common changes include: noticing and amending small errors; adjusting the word count (see below); dealing with repetition, and recognising the need for greater clarity in places.

Write your second draft incorporating all the improvements you have noted.

At this stage, it is useful to get a second opinion. You could ask a critical friend to read this second draft. Ideally, your tutor could read it to reassure you that you are on the right lines.

Amend your second draft in the light of any useful feedback you have been given.

6. Word Adjustment

Check the number of words you have produced. If your assignment is too short, think about which parts would benefit from further clarification or discussion. If your assignment is too long, delete any repetitions or wasted words. Pruning nearly always improves clarity and style. See page 106. Now write the final version.

7. The Final Check

Have a final check through including checking your citations and reference list (see the checklists in the appendix). Complete the submission sheet if your department uses these. Hand it in on time or by an agreed (negotiated) extension date.

A Good Assignment: Gaining Good Grades

There are seven key characteristics which any good essay will exhibit. When an assessor marks your work they will tend to award marks on the basis of the presence or absence of these characteristics. You will be gaining or shedding marks toward your grade largely in relation to these salient aspects of good work. However, be aware that different assessors may have differing responses to an essay, partly because there is, inevitably, a subjective element in marking, but also partly because the relative importance of these characteristics of good work will vary for individual assessors. Assessors will be guided by the marking criteria, however, so take account of this. In addition, where possible, if your tutor is the assessor, notice his or her preferences or foibles.

The Key Characteristics

1. Evidence of wide and relevant reading. Knowledge of the literature (see Chapter 1).
2. Good organisation of material (see Chapter 2).
3. Sound argument and use of relevant research (see Chapter 3).
4. Evidence of critical thinking (see Chapter 4).
5. Inclusion of analysis (see Chapter 5).
6. Originality (see Chapter 6).
7. Professional presentation and correct use of academic conventions (see Chapter 7).

Chapters 8 and 9 cover additional characteristics of other forms of assignment including oral presentations.

What Went Wrong: The Corresponding Seven Common Essay Errors

Unsurprisingly, the most common errors students make in writing an essay occur because one or more of the key characteristics of a good essay are not met. Again, your assessor will mark you down for committing these mistakes. Let us revisit our key characteristics and see how things go wrong.

1. The Literature

- No reference is made to the work of other writers, thinkers, researchers.
- Your own ideas are swamped by too many references and overlong quotations.
- The works chosen are irrelevant.

For example, in an essay entitled: 'What is Tourette Syndrome?' the focus must be on this condition. We do not need a lengthy account, as distinct from a mention, of all the co-morbidities that can be associated with Tourette Syndrome.

- Wrong attributions of ideas/research.

For example, do not attribute Darwin's actual ideas to a commentator, or the commentator's own slant on evolution to Darwin.

- The references are not correctly placed in the text nor correctly set out in the reference list. See section on References on page 110.

2. Organisation of Material

- Failing to answer the question and all parts of the question
- Poor essay structure
- No use of headings
- Poor introduction and overview
- No logical development
- Poor conclusion
- Too many or too few words (i.e. not staying within specified word limit)

3. Reasons and Evidence

- Too assertive. No arguments advanced for the claims made or counter arguments to arguments that are made against your claims. (By claims, here, we mean the propositions you are putting forward as valid, and by arguments, we mean the reasons and evidence you cite in support of your claims.)
- No relevant research cited in support.

4. Critical Thinking

All the material is descriptive with very little in the way of theories, critical questioning, distinctive critiques and critical reflection.

5. Forms of Analysis

There is little or no critical analysis – no meta-analysis, analysis of key concepts, no exploration of relevant theoretical material. Meta-analysis means taking an overview of your material in order to be critically reflective about it (see Chapter 5).

6. Point of View and Original Elements

- The student tells us what other writers think about the topic/question but does not give (or support) their own point of view.

We have tended to use 'claim' for any proposition you put forward as true. Your point of view is your perspective or stance on an issue. You add interest, too, by including your own examples or by drawing on your own experience.

7. Presentation and Academic Conventions

- The presentation is poor – poorly typed and not in accordance with departmental guidelines. (If your department does not have guidelines, choose a clear, sensible font such as Times New Roman or Arial, set appropriate (wide enough) margins and set line spacing to 1.5 or double line spacing.)
- The English is poor – unclear sentences, poor punctuation, spelling and grammar. (Use your software's inbuilt spellchecker to correct any spelling and grammar. If English is not your first language, there are lots of ESL (English as a Second Language) resources online with practical exercises and advice and tips that will help you to improve your writing.)
- Referencing and other academic conventions are applied incorrectly and inconsistently. See Chapter 7 for detailed information about academic conventions and referencing systems such as Harvard, which is often used in humanities subjects, the Vancouver system, which is used in medical and scientific papers and APA (the American Psychological Association style), often used in the social sciences.

Take Seven Steps to a Better Grade

Earlier, we identified seven steps to completion. We have also seen that the characteristics of a good essay, and the corresponding common errors, can be conveniently grouped into seven key areas. The first seven chapters of the book cover these key areas. Follow the advice in every chapter and you will achieve a good grade. What follows is a detailed explanation of the contents of each chapter. If you work your way through them, you will avoid the most common pitfalls.

If you fail to complete an assignment you will not obtain a grade – even a lowly one! This is why our introduction has discussed getting started, how to overcome writer's block and how to complete your assignment on time. Always remember that if you must rush to finish, or you fear you have gone wrong in some way, you have options. You could ask your tutor for extra time. You could hand your work in anyway and be prepared to be asked to resubmit. Ask for advice. Discuss what went wrong and clarify what you need to improve for any resubmission.

Chapter 1: Using the Literature

Students go wrong here in one of two ways. Either they make no use of the work of others ('no evidence of wide and relevant reading') or they cram in so many long quotations that there is no space for their own voice and their own ideas. That is why in this chapter you will learn how to identify the most relevant literature, and examples are given of too little, too much and a balanced use of the literature.

Chapter 2: Planning, Structure and Organisation

Poor assignments often show a lack of structure. There may be much irrelevant material. The assignment reads as though the student is writing down a stream of academic consciousness or taking a scattergun approach to the topic, i.e. throwing material onto the page in a random manner. To make a good plan is important because it will give your assignment structure and coherence. Good organisation of relevant material is one of the keys to a higher grade. Good organisation will also ensure that you produce a good introduction and an appropriate conclusion with logical order of material in the body of the essay and the helpful use of subheadings.

Chapter 3: Rational Thinking

Chapter 3 explains what we mean by rationality; it gives you the skills of reason giving, good argument and supporting your work with strong evidence.

A common error is to make sweeping claims that go beyond your evidence or to make unsupported statements and arguments. The name of the academic game is to have good reasons and/or evidence for your arguments and ideas. Don't earn a 'too assertive' comment, it will lead to some loss of marks.

Chapter 4: Critical Thinking

Chapter 4 explains what we mean by critical thinking; it gives you the skills of asking critical questions and engaging in critical reflection. These skills will ensure that your assignment will contain sufficient critical content to avoid the common error of being 'too descriptive'. A degree of criticality is often what separates pass level work from a 'good' or 'excellent' assessment.

Chapter 5: Analytic Thinking

Chapter 5 explains what we mean by analysis; including conceptual analysis, meta-analysis, philosophical reflection and metacognition. It will give you the skills to engage in these four forms of analysis.

Chapter 6: Originality

A good assignment will be well presented, make good use of the literature, provide reasons and evidence for its assertions and contain some critical/analytic thinking. A very good or excellent assignment will have a distinct point of view or a fresh perspective. In other words, it will have a touch of originality, which lifts it out of the pile! This is not as difficult to achieve as it may sound. Advice and examples are covered in Chapter 6. Never be afraid to produce your own slant on the topic (perhaps by drawing on your own personal or professional experience), provided that you give reasons for what you are suggesting.

Chapter 7: Presentation

Students are often marked down for poor presentation or for incorrect use of academic conventions or for many small errors. If you have comments like: *poor presentation, poor use of English, spoiled by small errors, incorrect referencing, poor use of quotations* and so on, take the advice in this chapter to heart. These kinds of errors do not necessarily lead you to fail, unless they are very bad or very numerous, but they do give a bad impression and tend to lead to a lower grade. Therefore, you can raise your grade simply by getting these more mechanical requirements completely correct. Similarly, if you follow academic conventions on such things as referencing, acronyms, good layout of tables and figures, etc. you will ensure a more polished and professional presentation and gain credit for this.

Chapter 8: Other Forms of Assignment

Reviews need to clearly convey the key information about the book (or presentation, etc.) under review, but will also need to critique this, using some of the techniques explored in Chapters 4 and 5. Students often fail to be sufficiently critical. (Remember, that to be critical includes highlighting positive as well as negative aspects of the item under review.) Both strengths and weaknesses need to be considered and evaluated.

    Reports of various kinds are sometimes given to students as an alternative to an essay. Clarity and conciseness are important for constructing a report. Students often fail to include all the important information. Tips on how to identify the important issues and details and how to structure the material using helpful headings are included in this chapter.

    This chapter also touches on group work, research projects, reflective journals, abstracts and summaries, and portfolios.

Chapter 9: Oral Presentations

Understandably, you may be nervous about giving an oral presentation and this can mar your performance. We have known situations where better material, nervously presented, has received a lower grade than poor material presented with confidence and conviction. You can use humour or anecdote to keep audience attention. PowerPoint presentations can be very helpful. All this is further explored in Chapter 9.

Conclusion

In this introduction we have explained that this book is for all students who wish to write good essays. Each chapter is devoted to helping you to develop useful HE skills and avoid the most common errors and pitfalls. The introduction also has advice on overcoming writer's block and has provided you with seven key steps to achieving a better grade.

Summary of Key Points

1. This book will help you to write your first essay or to get better grades than you achieved for previous ones. You will learn how to write a good essay at a level appropriate for higher education.
2. You are capable of completing a good essay or other assignment, but you were not born knowing what is required. This book will show you.
3. To avoid writer's block, write in bite-size chunks. Do not sit down intending to write the whole essay. Follow your plan (see Chapter 2). Remember it is only a first draft. Once you have a first draft it is easier to improve it.
4. Begin with a focus on the essay title. What is it asking from you? How many parts does it have? Now do the relevant reading. Use your recommended reading list. (There are some suggested search tools in Chapter 1.)
5. Read your first draft and note where it could be improved, e.g. correct small errors, cut repetitions, clarify any unclear text.
6. To adjust the word count: if the essay is too short, which parts would benefit from further discussion? If the essay is too long, delete any unnecessary words (e.g. very) and any repetitions.
7. Ask a critical friend to read your second draft and take on board any useful advice they offer.
8. A good essay must show:

    *   Evidence of wide and relevant reading. Knowledge of the literature (see Chapter 1)

        o   Common error: No citation of other writers or too many quotes from others.

    *   Good organisation of material (see Chapter 2)

        o   Common error: Haphazard, unstructured material, perhaps missing an introduction or a conclusion.

    *   Sound argument and use of relevant research (see Chapter 3)

        o   Common error: Assertive essay with no justifications given.

    *   Evidence of critical thinking (see Chapter 4)

        o   Common error: No critical questioning or reflection.

    *   Inclusion of analysis (see Chapter 5)

        o   Common error: No use of any of the forms of analysis, e.g. no definition of key terms.

    *   Originality (see Chapter 6)

        o   Common error: No inclusion of your point of view.

    *   Presentation and academic conventions (see Chapter 7)

        o   Common errors: Poor English, incorrect use of academic conventions such as acronyms and references.

A Preliminary Note: 'Voice'

Before we look at the skills covered in the following chapters, we are providing a preliminary note about deciding in which voice to write your essays. The voice you choose may vary according to the essay topic, and sometimes according to the preferences of your tutor/department.

You could write your essay in the first person (I would argue...) or in a less personal style, the third person, (the author would argue...) or in the passive voice (It could be argued that...).

Examples of first person:

In my view...

I suggest that...

Examples of the third person, less personal 'voice':

In the author's view...

The author would suggest that...

Examples of the passive 'voice':

One plausible view is...

It could be suggested that...

Which tone is to be preferred might, arguably, depend on the essay or assignment task. Some assignments would be too contrived if the direct 'I' were avoided. For example:

In addition to writing your five thousand word essay, write five hundred additional words reflecting on your own learning from writing your essay. (Such reflection is sometimes referred to as metacognition – an analytic task discussed in Chapter 5.)

We (the authors of this book) clearly use the direct, more informal first person, but we know that some university teachers prefer essays in the more formal, passive 'voice'. We would argue that the first person approach is more direct, less contrived, more involving for the reader and rather easier to write. Other academics would claim that this approach is less objective in tone and that students should be encouraged to be objective. Moreover, they believe that essays call for formality and that students should be able to write in the passive voice.

The important thing for you is to check with the tutor who has given you the essay. Do they have a view on this? Some university departments will have essay and assignment guidelines which include attention to this issue. Find out if your department provides such guidance. If so, follow the guidelines! In general, essays in the natural sciences are less likely to be acceptable in the first person than those in the social sciences.

> **Top Tip**
>
> Before you write your essay, check any department guidelines and ask your tutor about the acceptability (or otherwise) of using the first person in your work. Also check the word allowance, the hand-in deadline, marking criteria and any special requirements.

1

The Literature

Identifying and Using Relevant Key Books and Papers

Overview

- Introduction
- Why Use the Literature?
- Strategies, Tips and Tools for Identifying the Relevant Literature
- Define the Essay Question
- Use Keyword Searches
- Libraries and Online Databases
- Organise and Categorise Your Literature Review Information
- The Literature: An Area Full of Potential Pitfalls
- Moving from Pitfalls to Progress
- Use of the Literature
- Sample Essay: Choose Three Health Care Professions and Outline What You Consider to be the Core Skills of Each
- Sample Essay: Occupational Therapy and Skill – (Too much use of the literature)
- Sample Essay: Occupational Therapy and Skill – (Too little use of the literature)
- Sample Essay: Occupational Therapy and Skill – (A balanced use of the literature)
- Negative and Positive Approaches
- Conclusion
- Summary of Key Points
- References

Introduction

In this chapter you will learn how to identify and then make a balanced use of the literature relevant to your essay question. You will learn about tools that will help you to search the literature and the sample essays will show you what counts as a balanced use. Good use of the literature is crucial for achieving a high grade in your essays. The word 'literature' in this context is comprehensive in scope, covering books, articles in journals, the mass media, professional publications, Internet sources, etc.

Read Some Books!

Before you begin your essay you need to do some focused reading. Ask yourself what are the key books in the field. There is more on how to identify these later in this chapter. Read as much as time allows and do so critically (see Chapters 3, 4 and 5). You need to become familiar with your local and/or university library and how it classifies and stores its material. The library staff are there to help you and will not be surprised that you do not know your way around the shelves or the online databases and digital resources. A book published in several reprints shows that it is a widely read text. Look at the introduction, the content list and the index to see whether the book is relevant to your essay. Don't get bogged down by the sheer number of books on a topic. Select those relevant to your essay. Scanning the contents, and reading the preface, foreword, introduction and information on the jacket can save you time in your selection process. Bibliographies will also give you a further indication of the sources and topics covered in the book. Books will be creditable if they are on your recommended reading list or often cited by other writers, and published by reputable publishers. You can evaluate them using the CRAAP Test, which is a series of questions about Currency, Relevancy, Authority, Accuracy and Purpose (http://www.csuchico.edu/lins/handouts/eval_websites.pdf).

Using Journals and Professional Publications

Articles being shorter than books may be more focused to the essay question as well as quicker to read. They may be a bit daunting as they tend to be written for other academics and thus, for example, may use difficult terms and ideas without explanation. It may be that such articles are best read after an introductory book on the topic. Journals are reputable if they have sound editorial boards which include academics from established universities.

Evaluate the Mass Media

Documentaries and newspaper articles on your essay topic may be informative. You must evaluate the information and claims they contain against other sources of information.

Use the Internet with Caution

The Internet is useful provided you use it critically. Information is easily accessible, but is not always correct. Use it as a supplement for (and check it against) more reliable sources of information such as articles in peer-reviewed journals and reputable books or to carry out your initial searches. The Internet can be a portal to scholarly and peer-reviewed articles through Google Scholar. 'Peer reviewed' means that the articles have been scrutinised by several experts in the field. Reputable books are published by established publishers with a track record of publishing well-regarded, well-referenced books written by authors with relevant experience.

Do exercise some caution when using sources from the Internet such as social media channels, blogs and websites, as not all these sources contain valid or even accurate information. If you do use a source from the Internet, remember to cite this correctly (see Chapter 7 on citations and referencing).

Why Use the Literature?

Show Evidence of Wide and Relevant Reading

Your essay should show that you have some knowledge and understanding of the key literature relevant to the essay topic. Think for a moment about why students are given essays and assignments. There is both a learning and an 'assessment of learning' objective. Writing an essay is a learning journey. You learn, in an important area of your chosen discipline – an area encapsulated in the essay question. Reading for the essay you learn the accepted facts from established research, the key questions and concepts, the key ideas and theories, who the influential thinkers are and what they have said. It is from reading and thinking about what you read that you will gain knowledge and understanding in your chosen field of study.

In writing an essay you will also learn to organise your thoughts about a relevant topic, to begin to distinguish the important from the peripheral, to develop your own views and ideas and to develop your analytic academic skills.

In addition to this learning, the essay also provides a means by which your tutor can feed back to you, your developing strengths and your remaining weaknesses. Both you and your tutor have a means of monitoring your progress, and your tutor can be assured that you are gaining knowledge and understanding of the literature in your field of study.

For all these reasons it is important that your essay reflects some knowledge of the literature in your chosen field – knowledge gained from relevant reading.

Strategies, Tips and Tools for Identifying the Relevant Literature

There are a number of key steps to undertaking a literature review. These include defining the essay question so that your literature searches are relevant, and using the tools and techniques available to help you carry out your searches effectively and efficiently, and organise and categorise the information you gather into a coherent structure that you can refer back to throughout the period of your study.

Define the Essay Question

Each essay you write will have one or more direct or implicit questions that you will analyse and reflect on before you set about answering the question. During this process you will start to identify the key themes and topics you are writing about and this, in turn, will help you to identify the relevant literature you need to read.

There are several methods you can use to unpack and expand the themes and topics. One that you may already be familiar with is mind mapping, which was made popular by Tony Buzan (2002). Mind mapping is a visual technique that will help to uncover the key themes and topics as well as help you to establish any useful links and connections between them, which will also be useful during your planning.

There are numerous ways you can use mind mapping tools depending on your preferred methods and styles of working. A very simple mind map can be created using a blank sheet of paper and some coloured pens to colour code your mind map. Starting in the centre of the page, write your key question or concept and circle. Then draw lines out from this central idea to form branches, at the end of which you write the key themes and topics. The finished product will be your visualisation of your research question with all the relevant information you need to start your literature search.

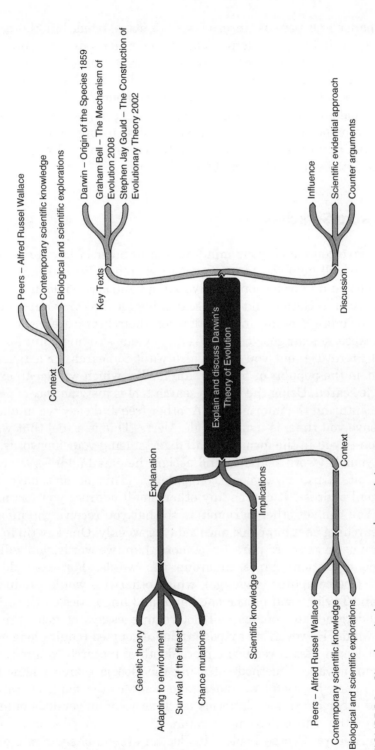

FIGURE 1.1 Simple mind map – essay key points

Using paper and pens is an easy way to get started, but there are also digital tools available online (often free) if you prefer a digital representation of your mind map. The simple example in Figure 1.1 uses Coggle.it (a Google Chrome extension). Digital mind maps can be stored and accessed from various devices including PCs, tablets and mobile phones.

You can make your mind maps as simple or as complex as you like. It will depend on your preferred style of working and learning. Since not everyone likes to use a mind map, you could simply brainstorm and write down keywords associated with each part of the question.

Use Keyword Searches

Once you have completed your mind map, a number of keywords will have emerged that will help you to narrow your searches. With technology being so ubiquitous, and information readily to hand and accessible, most students these days turn to Google and other search engines to carry out preliminary research, including finding information for their literature review. Google Scholar (https://scholar.google.co.uk) is an obvious starting point for credible sources of literature, but you might also want to search for articles, blogs, videos, etc. in the popular or mainstream media, which will mean extending your Google search. Using the Google search tool is just one way of doing this and then capturing the information. Another free and easy technique, which will also save you time, is using Google Alerts. This is a tool that will bring information to you in the form of email digests using your keywords.

Set up your keyword searches and assign the email address for receiving the alerts at https://www.google.co.uk/alerts. (This doesn't have to be a Google email address. It can be any other email address you use more frequently.) You can set other parameters so that you receive the information you are searching as it happens, once a day or weekly. One key tip to remember is if you use a keyword phrase, i.e. more than two words, you will need to use double quotation marks to group the words. For example: "Swift Language" (the computer language), which otherwise would produce alerts for birds and Taylor Swift on the one hand, and linguistics on the other.

Most undergraduate courses will not require essays of more than a few thousand words. However, many postgraduate courses require longer assignments. For longer essays requiring more depth of research, you may want to employ more advanced methods of using the Google search engine tools. It would, therefore, be useful to understand some of the main operators that Google and other electronic platforms (such as your university's online databases) use for this, called Boolean operators. They are named after the inventor of Boolean Algebra, George Boole. This logical system of searching electronic

TABLE 1.1   Using Boolean operators in search engines

Use double quotation marks to refine your search. Enclosing these terms in quotation marks means that Google will pick up the exact search term. Otherwise, you will end up with information on wolf and on conservation, etc.	"wolf conservation" "wolf biology" "wolf ecology" "wolf behavior"
Use the AND operator if you want to search for specific information that will link your subjects.	wolves AND Bulgaria wolves AND "prey density"
Use of OR means that at least one of your search terms is required and Google will return information on one or all of your search terms.	"wolf conservation" OR "wolf biology" "wolf behavior" OR "wolf behaviour"
Use NOT if your search term is likely to bring results that you don't want. For example, if you want results on the canid version of wolves and not the English football club, then you would use the operator NOT.	wolves NOT football wolves NOT "Wolverhampton Wanderers"

sources enables you to refine searches using the operators as AND, OR and NOT. These are particularly useful if your search uses common or generic terms and keywords. For example, if you wanted to search for information on wolves, you might want to learn about their conservation or their biology or ecology and you would need to combine these terms into a 'search string' (see Table 1.1).

We have outlined some of the basic operators you can use. If you want to take this a little further, there are more advanced searching facilities that Google uses. Simply type www.google.co.uk/advanced_search into your search box.

Libraries and Online Databases

Using Google as an online search tool is only one method among many. Your university will also have an online database of academic journals, and you will also have access to external databases of academic journals through the online university portals. Your university library will provide you with a user ID and password for this.

Using your key themes, topics and keywords from your mind mapping exercise, you can carry out online searches of these databases to find the most relevant journals, book chapters and other sources of information. Take some time to familiarise yourself with the key journals you will need and assess how credible and relevant they are to your literature search. As explained above, they will be creditable if they are on your carefully chosen recommended reading list for example, and if they are often cited by other writers and published by well-known publishers with a track record of good books. They will have editorial boards which include academics from established universities.

Libraries themselves also continue to be storehouses of physical information, especially university libraries. They also help you to get into the right frame of mind for research. Librarians can help if you are struggling to find what you need and they are usually highly knowledgeable on a wide range of subjects or are able to point you in the right direction. With our increasing reliance on digital resources, it can be easy to forget how valuable a resource librarians can be, and how their experience can help you to reduce the time you need to navigate complex university library systems.

Organise and Categorise Your Literature Review Information

Reviewing the literature will be an ongoing process particularly for longer essays and dissertations. It will generate a lot of information and records that you will need to organise and categorise. As part of the mind mapping or brainstorming process, you will have identified the key themes and topics, and this will give you some structure for organising all the material under relevant headings (see earlier example). You will then need to make the decision as to whether you want to store your information manually or digitally. Organising your information manually simply requires a physical indexing system which can either be in a folder or series of folders, or using a box card index.

If you choose to use a card index system, these are available in various sizes with alphabetically organised dividers. The simplest way to use the card index system would be to put the authors' names in alphabetical order (see Figure 1.2).

Most students these days prefer to use digital tools, and there are a number of these available. Check with your department what software is available.

Front of Card

Brookfield, S. (1986)
Understanding and Facilitating Adult Learning. Milton Keynes: Open University Press.
(This card would then be filed under 'B' for Brookfield.)

Back of Card

Keywords:
• Critical thinking • Adult learning • Education
(You might also want to add additional information to the back of the card as an aide memoire.)

FIGURE 1.2   Using a card index system

These may be free to use or have just a small fee to pay. There are also an increasing number of free bibliography and citation tools available which you can find using a simple Google search.

For dissertations, which require more comprehensive referencing, you may also choose to use digital research software for your literature reviews. Your university or college library will be able to advise you. There are online articles available to help guide you through the steps for this.

Whatever methods and tools you use, make sure they are the best fit for the purpose. They are free or cost-effective, and they save you time and effort. Also make sure that you adopt a consistent way of working when filling in the information on your literature search. You may choose an alphabetical system for filing, but it would also be a good idea to be able to sort into categories too. Software tools will do this for you at the touch of a button, but a manual system will require a little more thought. Just remember that you will need to retrieve the information so the easier it is to be able to achieve this, the better.

The Literature: An Area Full of Potential Pitfalls

When Mal did her very first University essay as an 18-year-old student, she felt lucky that the topic was one she knew quite a lot about and which she had already thought about and discussed with people. She wrote with confidence. Her essay was the correct length and she knew she had argued well for her point of view. As she saw her roommate working through a pile of books on her desk, she felt smug that she had not had to rely on extraneous material! She was disappointed to receive a low grade. She still remembers the feedback comments. *Well written and well argued but you show no evidence of knowledge of the relevant literature and the views of others. You have not even considered the alternative points of view.* Thus, she learned the hard way that some reading is required.

Her roommate also received a low grade, even after a time extension. Her feedback was that she had used too many long quotations and uncritically reproduced the ideas of too many writers, failing to include her own ideas and point of view.

A good essay should have a balance between no use of the work of others and so much of the work of others that your own ideas, and even the point of the essay question, become swamped.

Drawing on the work of others and including it in your essay is necessary to show your wide and relevant reading, but, unfortunately, this is often done badly. These common errors and pitfalls are explained in what follows. Use your tutor and this book to avoid *learning the hard way*.

Common Pitfalls

Some of the most common pitfalls are listed below. These are followed by tips and tools to help you identify the relevant literature for a particular essay. The chapter ends with sample extracts from essays showing good and less good use of 'the literature'.

Only Use What Is Relevant

You need to identify and focus only on literature that is relevant to your assignment. It is easy to be side-tracked by interesting research and interesting theories which are only very loosely connected to the issues you are meant to be exploring. You can always use a reference to point to something linked and interesting but which is beyond the scope of your essay.

The Seminal Literature: Do Not Make a Glaring Omission

Some thinkers/writers/research is so directly relevant, influential, recognised and referenced that to omit it from your essay looks just that – a glaring omission. (It could be tactful not to omit your tutor/lecturer's work – if they are the assessor and if it is relevant!) For example, if your essay requires an historical perspective on special educational needs in the UK, it will be a serious omission not to include the Warnock Report, a well-known and influential government report in the field.

Do Not Over-Rely on Quotations

Do not take up a large portion of your allotted word allowance with long quotations from the work of others. Summarise your sources accurately but succinctly with the appropriate reference so that any reader can check that you have indeed been accurate and fair to the writer in question. Only use quotations when they are so pertinent, well expressed and succinct that the actual words are worth reproducing. Usually the words of others should be no more than 5% of your words overall and any individual quotes no more than five lines.

Do Not Neglect Your Own Point of View

Although it is important to show that you know and understand the important work most relevant to the assignment question, do not neglect to give your own answer to the essay question or your own view of the essay subject. This does not mean that your view has to be different to a relevant thinker's view. Indeed you can acknowledge that like X you would argue that Y because of Z. If you can add an additional argument of your own or some additional support drawing on your own experience, this will add some originality. Do not forget to mention the most influential alternative viewpoint(s), but you could show the weaknesses in it and in the arguments/research advanced in its favour. (This will add some criticality.)

Do Not Neglect 'The Literature'

For essays with a short word allowance, and for some kinds of assignment, such as personal reflections, you may not need to include more than one or two references to the work of others. However, you should attempt to have this small number. There are techniques for brief referencing. For example: 'This same experience is reported in the seminal work of X (X, 1980)' or 'this influential idea of "reflection-in-action" was introduced and discussed by Schön (1983)'.

Do Not Read Indiscriminately or for Too Long

In what follows you will be given tips and tools to avoid indiscriminate reading by knowing how to focus on the most *relevant* sources for *this particular essay*. You will also need to include the most influential, well-regarded and much referenced works. Some may have an early date and many will have the most recent, up-to-date research. The most recent ones show that you are keeping up with your developing area of knowledge. You will also need to start writing at the planned time (which will be in good time to meet your deadline)! Avoid the pitfall, discussed in the introduction, of using your reading as an excuse to procrastinate the writing of your essay!

Moving from Pitfalls to Progress

The pitfalls discussed above can be conveniently grouped as:

- irrelevance
- omission
- too little use of 'the literature'
- too much reliance on 'the literature'.

How can these be avoided?

Avoid the Pitfall of Irrelevance

With indiscriminate reading it is easy to fall into the pit of irrelevance. Your essay usually has to be of a prescribed length. You cannot afford to waste

11

words. Everything you write and all your references should be relevant to the essay title.

Consider the titles suggested in the introduction.

Explain and discuss the four aspects of Brookfield's Notion of Critical Thinking. Do you consider this to be an influential idea?

The central ideas inherent in this title are huge and multifaceted: 'thinking', 'criticality', 'influential'. You may well, with relevance, indicate that there are many other aspects of thinking, additional to Brookfield's, that are considered to be 'critical' by other important writers. You may well, with relevance, discuss others whose ideas closely link with Brookfield's. However, your central focus must be the four key aspects identified by Brookfield! Do not allow yourself to be side-tracked by other kinds of thinking (e.g. artificial intelligence, metacognition) or devote too high a proportion of the essay to another thinker's account of critical thinking. Your whole essay needs to keep Brookfield's four aspects (part one of the title) and the influence of his ideas (part two of the title) as the focus of the two parts of your essay, with any ideas and research from the literature drawn on as part of discussing this main focus. Of course, in discussing each of Brookfield's four aspects of critical thinking and in assessing their influence you should refer to other relevant work. Discussions which directly relate to one or more of Brookfield's aspects (in agreement or criticism) are relevant in discussion of the aspects. Ideas and developments which draw on Brookfield's ideas will be relevant in discussing the influence of his ideas.

Top Tip

Use the most relevant and the most referenced writers and of course Brookfield's own writing!

Avoid the Pitfall of Omission

Now consider the Darwin title.

Explain and discuss Darwin's theory of natural selection.

The literature about natural selection is vast. Discussion with references which a student might use for this essay might include: Books about Darwin (e.g. Browne (2007) *Darwin's 'Origin of Species': A Biography*) and books giving interpretations of his work (e.g. Reznick (2009) *The 'Origin' Then and Now:*

An Interpretive Guide to the 'Origin of Species'); books about natural selection (e.g. Williams (1992) *Natural Selection: Domains, Levels and Challenges*) or some aspect of it (e.g. Popper (1978) 'Natural selection and the emergence of mind'). This student could fail to directly draw on Darwin's own seminal *On the Origin of Species by Means of Natural Selection* (Darwin, 1859). To leave out the text central to an essay title will strike the assessor as a glaring omission! Yet this is not uncommon. Try to read the original key text and not just (the often simplified) commentaries. By all means use such more accessible explanations to help you to understand the central 'key' thinker.

Top Tip

Know, read and use the GIANTS in your field!

Avoid the Pitfall of too Little Use and of too Much Use of the Literature

In the sample assignments below, three pieces of work demonstrate too much use of the literature, too little use and a balanced use respectively.

Use of the Literature

We will consider a 3,000 word assignment for students on a Health and Social Care course and provide three examples of one section of this essay.

Sample Essay: *Choose three health care professions and outline what you consider to be the core skills of each*

It would be sensible to allow approximately 600 words for the introduction to this essay discussing the concept of skill in relation to health care and saying which three professions are to be discussed. It adds rigour if you can give a reason for choosing this particular three, perhaps because they are widely different from each other to give breadth or, alternatively, because they are linked in some crucial way or because these particular professionals often work in a care team.

It would be sensible to allow about 600 words for a conclusion, perhaps giving some of your own views about the degree to which there are common core skills, or about which skill is preeminent for all care professions, with your reasons for saying this.

(Continued)

(Continued)

Perhaps this skill is a prerequisite for the development of all other skills or is an essential aspect of being skillful in a caring role. It would be good to link your concluding thoughts to the conceptual discussions about 'skill' in the introduction and to the key points that have emerged in discussing the three professions. Each of the three sections on the three professions will need its own short conclusion and the essay as a whole will need its own longer (600 words) conclusion. All essays need a conclusion which should draw on the preceding material to round it off, often by actually drawing conclusions, giving (with reasons) your own point of view, or sometimes highlighting or summarising the key point/points of the essay as a whole.

To keep the essay balanced you will have approximately 600 words for each profession. You could divide the 1,200 words you have allowed yourself for the introduction and conclusion differently. (Perhaps 800 for the introduction and 400 for the conclusion). However, your essay will lack balance if you do not have both an introduction and a conclusion and will lack balance if you devote substantially more (or less) words to one of the three professions than to the other two.

Suppose you choose Occupational Therapy as one of the three professions to be discussed. Below are three samples of:

- 'Six hundred' words overwhelmed by the literature (with many deliberate mistakes)
- 'Six hundred' words making too little reference to the literature
- 'Six hundred' words making good use of relevant literature

Sample Essay: *Occupational therapy and skill –* (too much use of the literature)

The specific occupational skills for an occupational therapist relate to a focus on human occupation and activity analysis and adaptation of activity or occupation (Kielhofner Forsyth 2009). In his book about skills in occupational therapy ES Duncan also points out this need for considerable analysis

More explanation needed.

'Practitioners spend a lot of time thinking, judging/assessing, collaborating with clients, making decisions and reflecting on what they have done. Yet how often, and for how long, do people spend time to stop and consider why they made certain decisions, on what evidence they base their decisions, how successful their strategy of collaborating with clients is, and how evidence based their judgments in practice are? These skills are central, yet largely invisible to competent and sensible practice.' (2009:)

Rather a long quotation.

The focus on human occupation means that occupational therapy can sometimes be a catalyst for social action and change. (Kielhofner, 2008) This links and works in partnership with other care professions which is itself a strength.

More explanation needed.

This emphasis on doing also links with other care professions. Comparison with other professions in healthcare services – for example nursing, psychology or social work – may reveal that there is potential overlap with other care professions. There are key core skills which may be attributed to a number of the care professions; for example a person-centered approach, empowerment, assessment of needs, care planning, goal setting and evaluation (DH 2004, BAOT 2010, BASWA 2012).

✓

There are a variety of different models for practicing occupational therapy. Hammel (2014) discusses these, showing that there are differences of philosophy between them. She includes Iwama (2006), who takes a Japanese perspective. This links with Fidler and Fidler (1978), who mention 'becoming part of society'. she also mentions the influence of Maslow's hierarchy of needs (1987) and Wilcox (1998 and 2006) with her synthesis of 'doing, being and becoming'. Models such as these have been developed from research and aim to provide a clear theoretical framework and structure for clinical practice. The Model of Human Occupations (MOHO, see Kielhofner 2008) is now an accepted international occupational therapy model of practice, with a highly respected and rigorous evidence base. It is noted as 'Occupation focused, client-centered, holistic' (Kielhofner, 2008: p 56).

Relate all this to skills.

'MOHO is inherently a client centered model in two important ways;

- It views each client as a unique individual whose characteristics determine the rationale for the nature of the therapy goals and strategies.
- It views what the client does, thinks and feels as the central mechanism of change.' (Kielhofnr G, Forsyth K p 143).

It is part of the occupational therapists role to utilise the skills possessed by clients, to identify and develop these skills.

✓

Leadership is also a recognized key skill of occupational therapy (Duncan 2009, Barr 2008, COT 2009). Arguably occupational therapy's person-centred philosophy would best fit

(Continued)

(Continued)

with a collaborative model of leadership (Finlay, 1993). There is a group work element in this (Schwartzberg, 2009). Occupational therapists hold particular skills in group work (Creek 2003, COT, 2010, Finlay, 1993). Aristotle states that man is essentially a social animal, (cited in Aronsen, 1972). Humans are tribal by nature and they work and survive in groups. Occupational therapists in practice have concerns for people they think are isolated and have little contact with others. ✓

The occupational therapist must also learn to take account of the environment. This requires awareness of many aspects. ✓

'The environment can be defined as the particular physical and social, cultural, economic, and political futures of one's contexts that impact upon the motivation, organization, and performance of occupation.' (Kielhofner, 2008 p 86).

Health care practitioners, like other health care professionals, must make careful records of their work. ✓

'Health care practitioners make records of their interaction with people to ensure that the identified health and social care problems and needs are documented, together with resulting interventions and outcomes. In addition to individual care records, systems will be in place to record, anonymised information about care on a wider basis. It is essential that the occupational therapist understands, uses and contributes to these vital communication tools.' (Creek J, Lougher, L 2008) *Another long quote. This could be in your own words.*

Even with the variety of models of practice with their different underlying philosophies there seems to be a number of core skills, often shared with other professionals, which come through in all of these different models and philosophies. These skills have been mentioned, namely, practical skills in 'doing', analysis, leadership skills and group work skills. *A good succinct conclusion, though the point could have been more fully developed.*

(732 Words)

Comments

This student has gone over the allocated 600 words. She has used over 20 references to other writers and used four long quotations. Not all citations are included in your reference list and some of the details are incorrect. Almost one third of the piece comprises the words of others! (As an assessor for a distance learning course Mal was advised that direct quotations should not be more than 5% of the student's work. Whilst this might be a little over stringent for some kinds of essay, clearly 33% allows too little space for

the writer's own words and ideas) The writer is clearly a conscientious student who has read very widely, but she seems to be
overwhelmed by her reading and determined to drag it all in –
partly digested, rarely explained with clear links to the skills
required by the work of the occupational therapist. The student
believes that leadership skills and skill in group work are crucial
but does not explain why. She mentions activity analysis and the
development of client skills but does not discuss analytic or
educational skills. She sometimes loses sight of the main
requirement to say what the core skills are by showing their
relevance to occupational therapy.

In her final paragraph, she makes the interesting claim that
some skills are so central to occupational therapy that they are
recognized in all the different models of practice. If the student
had explored this idea more fully, giving good reasons for the
claim, this would have made an original and critical dimension
to the piece.

If this piece is a reflection of the entire essay the student
would have been given either a fail, or, more likely because of
the evident wide reading and some good points, a resubmission. To have achieved a higher grade she could have:

(i)   Used her own words to more succinctly make the points
      made in the long quotations.
(ii) The words saved could have been used to explain her key
      points more fully and to give reason for the interesting claim
      made in the final paragraph.

-0-0-0-

Sample Essay: *Occupational therapy and skill* – (too little use of the literature)

Occupational therapy is 'the use of assessment and treatment to
develop, recover or maintain the daily living and work skills of people with a physical, mental or cognitive disorder' (BLS). Clearly this
is such a broad remit that considerable knowledge and empathy,
and a wide range of skills will be relevant. The assessment
involved will require considerable skills of analysis and to provide
the treatment will require many practical skills and people skills.

(Continued)

(Continued)

Occupational therapists focus much of their work on identifying and eliminating environmental barriers to independence and to participation in daily activities. *(REF)* Again skills of analysis are involved, in assessing, reviewing and evaluating needs as well as the barriers to fulfilling those needs.

Give examples of environmental barriers and give a reference.

Occupational therapy practice is client centred practice that focuses on the clients own perceived needs and interests *(REF)*.

Occupational therapists often work closely with other professionals such as physiotherapists, speech therapists, nurses and social workers. Clearly being able to cooperate with others in competent team work will require group work skills *(REF)*.

It is perhaps insufficiently recognised that since new skills are to be developed in the client, the occupational therapist also acts as a teacher and coach. Educational skills of teaching and training are required.

In addition to all the high level skills, such as analytic skills and educational skills, the occupational therapist will also need the more basic skills of numeracy and literacy since she will need to write reports and keep records and draw up budgets.

Give a reference. √

The occupational therapist seeks to help clients to develop occupational skills for a successful and fulfilling daily life. This calls for a high level of empathy. Empathy is the ability to enter into and share the feelings of another. I suggest that this skill is a crucial one. It is required for a truly client-centred approach. It facilitates good analysis of the client's needs from the client's point of view. Given the nature of all care work, empathy is an important skill for all health care professionals. It is therefore a core skill for occupational therapy and one shared with the other care professionals with whom the occupational therapist works. √

Give a reference.

√

(360 Words)

Comments

The student who wrote this produced a well-structured piece of work and makes sensible points e.g. educational skills as undervalued and empathy as crucial. This student is much more in control of her material than student one. However, no use is made of 'the literature'. I have indicated, in italics, potential reference points. These would have pointed to fuller discussion and support of the point being made. Thus good references to relevant reading would have given this piece more depth and rigour.

This piece reads as the work of an intelligent student who has not put too much reading and preparation into her work. If the piece is a reflection of the essay as a whole she would probably receive a pass which with more depth through reading the key literature could have been a high grade. She uses 240 less words than the 600 allocated. She could have used the additional words, given her emphasis on empathy, to argue that this is indeed a skill as distinct from, say, a disposition or an emotion. This would have given an original element and a distinct point of view. Some of the additional words could also have been used to explore the writing of others at relevant points, for example on environmental barriers or on team work, group skills or on educational skills. In short, to achieve a higher grade this student could have

(i)   drawn on the literature at relevant points.
(ii) made use of the spare words to support her own claims.

-0-0-0-

Sample Essay: *Occupational therapy and skill –* (a balanced use of the literature)

At the heart of occupational therapy lies a therapeutic notion of 'occupation'. This is not the dated conception of simply occupying the time of vulnerable people with arts and crafts but is valuing occupation, 'doing', as intrinsic to the nature and needs of human beings. This simple word 'doing', however, covers all the many daily living, leisure and work skills needed by the clients. This is expressed by The Bureau Of Labour Statistics as 'the use of assessment and treatment to develop, recover or maintain the daily living and work skills of people with a physical, mental or cognitive disorder' (BLS). *A good opening.*

Clearly the breadth of this definition, encompassing assessment and treatment skills across a huge range of therapeutic needs (physical, mental and cognitive), will require that the occupational therapist has an equally broad range of skills.

To have analytic skills requires that the occupational therapist is able to reflect clearly and to be self-critical in making assessments. Such assessments include making balanced judgments, decision making, goal setting, problem solving and finding

(Continued)

19

(Continued)

and appraising evidence. To improve analysis and practice, they must be a 'reflective practitioner' critically reflecting on their practice before, during and after it (Schön, 1987).

Add to this that occupational therapists must take account of environmental and cultural factors. 'The environment can be defined as the 'particular physical and social, cultural, economic, and political features of ones contexts that impact upon the motivation, organisation and performance of occupation.' (Kielhofner, 2008: 86). This adds considerably to the complexity of the analyses of needs.

Occupational therapy is widely considered to be a client centred practice (Sumsion, 2006). This requires that the occupational therapist is able to understand the client's needs from the client's own point of view and therefore must develop a trusting partnership. Thus people skills are also required. The ability to understand 'need' from the client's point of view is part of 'caring' about that person as an individual with their own wishes and perspectives. A humanistic emphasis on care is implicit in the term 'health care professional' and thus people skills should be part of practice for all health care professionals.

Group skills are also required by the occupation therapist, both the group skills required by working with other professionals and those required by working with therapeutic groups. In team work with other professionals, the occupational therapist can engage in group critical reflection. This provides an opportunity for improved practice through shared discussion, leading to enriched perspectives. (McKay, 1900)

Having discussed a number of crucial, complex skills it should also be mentioned that basic skills of numeracy and literacy are also required by occupational therapists. They must record identified needs, interventions made and outcomes achieved.

Finally, I suggest that at the heart of the occupational therapist's role are the educational skills. The emphasis in occupational therapy is on equipping clients with useful skills for the activities they need to do or which they will find fulfilling. Therefore, the occupational therapist needs educational skills of teaching and training to encourage and develop their clients' range of skills. They need to know how to do these tasks themselves and how to teach or coach their clients in this 'doing'. This will give clients self-confidence as they become more self-reliant. Whereas all health care professionals need people skills, basic skills, analytic

√
Good link to the literature.

A useful brief quotation.

A good link to skills.

Two kinds of group skills – good.

Good paragraph.

skills and some educational skill, nevertheless, this educative role with its focus on **occupation** is the distinguishing feature of occupational therapy.

Your own point of view, well supported. Good.

To conclude, a closer look at skills for occupational therapy shows that the perception of this role as merely about occupying the time of impaired people is woefully inadequate! To give impaired clients skills which will be therapeutic has huge implications about what occupational therapy involves.

(618 Words)

A good conclusion linking to the introduction and the essay emphasis on skill.

Comments

This piece, like the second piece is well structured and well written. Both have a 'point of view'. One highlights 'empathy' and the other 'educational skills'. Both give reasons for their claims and, given the limited word allowance of 600 words, both cover much ground. (In 600 words, one cannot be fully comprehensive.) However, through judicious references to relevant literature the third student shows familiarity with written work on occupational therapy and its skills and practice. This adds breadth to the piece, allowing the indication that beyond the scope of 600 words there is more that could be and has been said. It also adds depth and rigour since the references allow the student to succinctly indicate key issues and authors whose work supports what is being said by the student. Assuming the same level in the rest of the essay this piece, with its balanced use of the literature, would receive a high grade.

Negative and Positive Approaches

If you do not follow the advice of this chapter on good use of the literature you may see comments from your tutor, as part of his/her feedback, like the ones below. These point to the most common errors in this area: neglecting references to the literature in the essay or in one part of the essay; using too many long quotations; lack of a relevant, accurate reference list.

Sample Negative Comments

- There is evidence of relevant reading for part A of the essay but no attempt to reference the relevant work for part B.
- You use too many long quotations. Use your own words more often and reference the source of the ideas.

- You have read widely but have made an odd selection from the available literature. The books you use are outdated and the few papers you have cited are largely irrelevant.
- You show evidence of wide and relevant reading but have failed to produce a corresponding reference list.
- It is a pity that having produced a well-written and well-referenced essay, you have produced an inaccurate and inconsistently laid out set of reference details in your reference list. Use the reference system provided by your department consistently. If departmental guidelines are not provided, use the Harvard, or another well-regarded reference system.

Wide and relevant reading is demonstrated by making relevant reference to the work of others in support of your answer. In particular, you will include reference to key books and papers for your essay question. This reference to relevant books and papers shows that you have linked your own ideas to those of writers on your essay topic. Do not forget, as we have emphasised in this chapter, to show a good balance between your own ideas and the ideas and words (with short quotations) of others. This balanced use of the relevant literature will lead to positive comments like those set out below:

Sample Positive Comments

- There is evidence of wide reading which you have used well to support your argument. You have produced a strong and relevant reference list.
- You have used a small number of brief, well-chosen quotations drawn from the most relevant and well-regarded thinking in the field. You demonstrate knowledge of key books and papers most relevant to this essay question.
- As well as showing knowledge of the key books relevant to the essay you have included references to relevant papers and original material from your own background.
- You make good links between your own ideas and those of thinkers in the field.

Brief Exercise

Practise Three Voices

Write a short piece giving your view of the main advantages of books and journal articles respectively. Write this piece in the personal voice, the third person voice and the passive voice.

A Balanced Use of the Literature

Ask yourself:

- Why will too little use of the literature lose you marks?
- Why will too much use of the literature lose you marks?
- What is a balanced use of the literature?

Feedback is given in Appendix 4.

Conclusion

We have seen that showing evidence of wide reading will help you to achieve a high grade for your essays or assignments and have also seen how to try for a balanced use of the literature. Finding, reading and understanding relevant texts and using these to support your response to the essay question are key academic skills. You must develop these skills to achieve that high grade.

Summary of Key Points

1. To ensure that your essay achieves a pass, you must show evidence of some relevant reading, and for a high grade you must show your knowledge and understanding of more of the relevant literature. (You must reference this reading at the appropriate point in your essay – see Chapter 7.)
2. To write a good essay you must begin with some focused reading. Take advice on this from your tutor and draw on your recommended reading list.
3. Make notes as you read including the main contents of each book and paper, and record the details of author, title, date, place of publication, publisher. These details will be useful for your reference list.
4. Become familiar with your local and university libraries. The library staff are there to help you.
5. You can draw on books, papers in journals, the mass media, the Internet.
6. If you want to use mind mapping or search tools such as Boolean operators, read the first part of this chapter.
7. Only make use of material relevant to your essay question. Try to keep your reading focused and relevant, which means being selective in what you read.
8. Do not omit reference to the key thinkers on your essay topic. You could ask your tutor about this.
9. Do not use too many long quotations. Show your understanding of the writer by putting their ideas in your own words (then reference them).
10. Although your essay must show knowledge of other thinkers and writers, do not forget to say what **you** think about the essay question, giving your reasons.
11. The books and papers you have brought into your essay should be noted both in the text and in your reference list.
12. Finally, finding, reading and understanding relevant texts and using these to support your response to the essay question are key HE skills. You must develop these skills to achieve that high grade.

For chapter exercise feedback, further reading ideas and more tips on polishing your assignment, check out the appendices at the back of the book.

References

Aronson, E. (1972) *The Social Animal*. New York: Worth Freeman.

Barr, H. (1998) 'Competent to collaborate', *Journal of Inter-professional Care*, 12: 2.

British Association of Social Workers (BASW) (2012) Code of Ethics. Available at: https://www.basw.co.uk/codeofethics/.

Brookfield, S. (1987) *Developing Critical Thinkers. Challenging Adults to Explore Alternative Ways of Thinking and Acting*. San Francisco: Jossey-Bass.

Browne, J. (2007) *Darwin's 'Origin of Species': A Biography*. London: Atlantic Books.

Buzan, T. (2002) *How to Mind Map: The Ultimate Thinking Tool That Will Change Your Life*. London: Thorsens.

College of Occupational Therapists (BAOT) (2005) *COT/BAOT Briefing:/Integrated Care Pathways*. London: College of Occupational Therapists.

College of Occupational Therapists (COT) (2005) *College of Occupational Therapists' Code of Ethics and Professional Conduct for Occupational Therapists*. London: College of Occupational Therapists.

Creek, J. and Lougher, L. (eds) (2008) *Occupational Therapy and Mental Health* (4th edition). Edinburgh: Elsevier.

Darwin, C. (1859) *On the Origin of Species by Means of Natural Selection*. London: John Murray.

Department of Health (2004) *Knowledge and Skills Framework*. Available at: https://bmchealthservres.biomedcentral.com/articles/10.1186/1472-6963-4-15.

Duncan, E.S. (2009) *Skills for Practice in Occupational Therapy*. Edinburgh: Elsevier.

Fidler, G.S. and Fidler, J.W. (1978) 'Doing and becoming: Purposeful action and self-actualization', *American Journal of Occupational Therapy,* 32 (5): 305–10.

Forsyth, K. and Kielhofner, G.(2006) 'The model of human occupation; integrating theory into practice and practice into a theory', in E. A. S. Duncan (ed). *Foundations for Practice in Occuptional Therapy* (4th edition). Edinburgh: Churchill Livingstone. pp. 69–207.

Hammel, J., Finlayson, M. Kielhofner, G., Helfrich, C.A. and Peterson, E. (2001) 'Educating scholars of practice: An approach to preparing tomorrow's researchers', *Occupational Therapy in Healthcare*. IS 1/2 157-176.

Iwama, M.K. (2006) 'The Kawa (river) model: Nature, life flow, and the power of occupational therapy', in F. Kronenberg, S.S. Algado and N. Pollard (eds), *Occupational Therapy Without Borders: Learning From the Spirits of Survivors*. Edinburgh: Elsevier. pp. 213–27.

Kielhofner, C.G. and Forsyth, K. (2009) 'Activity analysis', in E. Duncan (ed.), *Skills for Practice in Occupational Therapy*. Edinburgh: Elsevier. pp. 91–103.

Maslow, A. H. (1962) *Towards a Psychology of Being*. Princeton: D van Nostrand Company.

McKay, E.A. (2008) 'Reflective practice: Doing, being and becoming a reflective practitioner', in E. Duncan (ed.), *Skills for Practice in Occupational Therapy*. Edinburgh: Elsevier. pp. 55–72.

Popper, K. (1978) 'Natural selection and the emergence of mind', *Dialectic,* (32): 339–55.

Reznick, D.N. (2009) *The 'Origin' Then and Now: An Interpretive Guide to the 'Origin of Species'*. Princeton, NJ: Princeton University Press.

Schon, D. A. (1987) *Educating the Reflective practitioner: Towards a New Design for Teaching and Learning in the Professions*. San Francisco: Jossey-Bass.

Sumsion, T. (ed.) (2006) *Client Centred Practice in Occupational Therapy: A Guide to Implementation* (2nd edition). Edinburgh: Elsevier.

Schwartzberg, S.I. (2009) 'Group skills for practice in occupational therapy', in E. Duncan (ed.), *Skills for Practice in Occupational Therapy*. Edinburgh: Elsevier. pp. 175–89.

Wilcox, A. (2006) *An Occupational Perspective of Health* (2nd edition). Thorofare, NJ: Slack.

Williams, G.C. (1992) *Natural Selection: Domains, Levels and Challenges*. Oxford: Oxford University Press.

2
Planning Your Essay

Overview

- Introduction
- The Importance of Planning
- How to Construct a Plan
- Negative and Positive Approaches
- Conclusion
- Summary of Key Points
- References

Introduction

In this chapter you will acquire the skills of planning and organising your work; skills which are vital in producing the well-structured essays and assignments required for the attainment of good grades. You will see how to construct a logical and helpful plan and learn about the many ways this will help you.

The Importance of Planning

If we were allowed to give you just one piece of advice or 'top tip' it would be this: plan out your essay before you write it.

You need to read from the texts recommended for this essay in order to deepen your understanding of the question and to begin to formulate your answer. You will then be able to construct a plan. Your plan may point to the need for some additional reading. However if you read beyond the early stages of your writing you may become overwhelmed and lose focus.

You will see in this chapter how you can construct a plan on one or, at most two, sides of A4, which will help you to:

- Produce a well-organised piece of work.
- Stick to your word allowance.
- Meet your deadline.
- Stay focused on the essay question.
- Cover all parts of the essay title.
- Produce an appropriate and interesting introduction.
- Include a rounded and satisfying conclusion.

In addition to all the benefits listed above, having a plan to follow will ensure that you do not inadvertently leave out key material and ideas which you had intended to include and will even ease you into getting started.

We find that when we plan a piece of work, finding the right structure for the material not only increases our *control* of it, it also develops our *understanding*. This increased understanding sometimes gives you insights, or allows you to see new connections, providing additional interest and originality.

Top Tip

Take control of your essay by starting with a plan.

How to Construct a Plan

Write to the Title

- Take that A4 sheet of paper and write the title of your essay very accurately at the top of the page.
- What is it requiring of you?
- How many parts does it have?
- Consider the literature you have been reading for the essay and the notes you have made. What material must you include?
- Reflect on what you want to say in response to the title.
- This title is often referred to as the essay question even when it is not in question form. All essays, and thus all titles, implicitly want your response – in a sense, your answer.

Check the Essay Requirements

Before you start your essay make sure that you know the following requirements for it. (If not check with your tutor.)

- Check the word allowance, the deadline, the 'voice' to use, the style requirements, the marking criteria and the learning outcomes.
- Ensure that your material will match the marking criteria and will cover the expected learning outcomes. Also ensure that you understand any particular requirements for this particular essay.

The Introduction

- Write 'introduction' at the beginning of your plan.
- Think about how you could introduce the topic or what background/context needs to be given. Or you may need to define the key terms or analyse the key concept. Or perhaps it would be useful for an essay question that is complex or many parted simply to set out, in order, what the essay will cover.
- Make some key notes on your plan to remind you of what your introduction will contain.
- Regard these notes for your introduction as provisional in that when you have completed your essay you may want to revisit the introduction and add to or amend it.

The Main Body of the Essay

- What should come first immediately after your introduction? If the essay has two parts what should begin the first part? Make a note of this – accompanied by bullet points or keywords.
- Go on to the development from your opening section. Again mark this by bullet points or a number of keywords.
- When the first part is completed, begin part two.
- Continue to structure your material in a logical sequence – noting key ideas, references and the research that each section of the sequence requires.

Think About the Conclusion

- Your final section will be a conclusion to the essay, which should not end abruptly but round off (conclude) in a satisfying way. Perhaps it could sum up the key points, or give your own point of view, or point out questions that remain unanswered, or actually draw some conclusions from what has been covered in the body of the essay.
- Finally you can, if it would be helpful, note the approximate number of words you will allocate for each section. The total words allotted will be equal to the word allowance for your essay as a whole. The word allocation is not set in stone. You may find one section

needs more words to explain and discuss its material than you had imagined and another section could be covered more briefly. However, having a rough guide to word allocation may help you to keep your material balanced, not, for example, finding you have used three-quarters of the essay word allowance before you reach the equally important second part of the essay question.

Similarly, you may find it helpful to note some time allowance for each section – dividing the time you have, for example nine weeks, up to the essay deadline, into sensible, approximate segments. Thus if you find that you have gone considerably beyond the time allowed for the introduction, for example, you will know that you must speed up (see Figure 2.1).

The following sample plans are designed to show you how to plan different kinds of essay questions, with appropriate, logical structures and how to include helpful notes to yourself (key ideas, key references, etc.).

Though the plan will help you to be organised and your material well structured, you may well find that additional ideas and connections occur to you as you write. Provided these are relevant, they need not be excluded just because they are not in the plan. Look at your plan to check where this new material should best be incorporated. For example, if you think a particular writer should not have been omitted, look at your plan to discover a link with his or her ideas and incorporate them (with references) here. If you have suddenly thought of another strong reason for the view you support, look at your plan for where you are arguing for your view. How important is your extra reason? Incorporate it as the first or last of your supportive reasons, according to its relative strength.

The following five plans include:

Plan One – A short, largely descriptive, introductory essay. (2,000 words)

Plan Two – A two-part expository essay with several sections in each part. (3,000 – 4,000 words)

Plan Three – An essay with a debate format. (5,000 words)

Plan Four – A discussion/persuasive essay. (5,000 – 6,000 words)

Plan Five – A self-reflective, multi-stranded, narrative essay. (7,000 words)

As has been mentioned earlier, essay titles are often referred to as the essay question, even though they are not all posed in the form of a question. This reference to the essay question highlights the need to reflect on what **you** think about the subject – your response or 'answer'.

Essay Writing plan

Task	week one	week two	week three	week four	week five	week six	week seven	week eight	week nine
1. Preparation Think about essay question and what is required consider resources needed and write these down Plan time required to complete essay	▓								
2. Literature search Allocate time for library and focused research Allocate reading time		▓	▓						
3. Planning Produce outline structure of the essay			▓						
4. Write first draft Find comfortable work space Allocate time for writing each day Allocate time for reading literature			▓	▓	▓	▓			
5. Complete second draft Does the essay flow? Are there any repetitions? Are there any sentences or paras that need rewriting? Get someone else to read through second draft							▓	▓	
6. word adjustment Check number of words Delete unnecessery words and phrases Is the essay long enough?								▓	
7. Final check Make use of checklist Check references and citations Complete submission sheet (if necessary) Check presentation Final check on word length Submit essay									▓

FIGURE 2.1 A sample timed writing plan

Essay One: A First Essay (in this case an introduction to study skills).
***Select two of the following sources of information and suggest
two advantages and two drawbacks in relation to each:
Books; journals; mass media; Internet.***

This 2,000 word essay might be given to students near the beginning of a course in any of the Social Sciences. Even in a brief essay an introduction and conclusion (albeit relatively brief ones) help to frame a response. A plan will also help to ensure that you do not omit one of the 'advantages' or one of the 'drawbacks'.

Tutor Assessment

Your tutor will want to see you demonstrate an understanding of the nature of each of these potential sources of information. They will want you to back up your claims about advantages and disadvantages with good reasons. You will gain marks for incorporating good points made by other writers (use of the literature) and also gain marks for your own ideas. If you can back up your claims with an example from your own learning, this will add originality (your own voice). Giving a reason at the outset for your selection of the two sources you choose to discuss will add to the 'rational' tone of your short, relatively descriptive essay. In the plan to follow, books and articles are chosen because these are the most prominent sources on the course reading list and are considered the most reliable sources. Reliable books are published by reputable publishers and written by authors with a relevant background. Journal articles are peer-reviewed, which means that at least two well-regarded academics will comment on the article to ensure they are of the right standard. If the student had chosen the Internet as one of the sources to write about, they could have pointed out that it is increasingly influential. If the mass media had been selected, the student could argue that they are more readily overlooked as a potential source of interesting material.

   A longer and more self-reflective essay on similar ground could be given towards the end of a course or module. (See Sample Plan Five.)
   Word Allocation (This is always approximate, provisional and revisable.)
   Plan One

–   You could allot 400 words for the advantages of each source = 800 words.
–   You could allot 400 words for the drawbacks of each source = 800 words.
–   You could allot 400 words shared between the introduction and conclusion
     = 400 words.

Total = 2,000 words.

Sample Plan One

Select two of the following sources of information and suggest two advantages and two drawbacks in relation to each: Books; journals; mass media; Internet.

Plan

Introduction

State choice (books and journals). Chosen because these are the most prominent sources on the course reading list and are considered the most reliable.

Books

Advantage One – A book provides a more sustained exploration of a subject, providing greater breadth of knowledge and understanding. (Give an example of a good introductory text.)

Advantage Two – A small number of key books can show you, through the works they discuss and reference, a network of relevant literature. (Illustrate the point by reference to reading to date.)

Drawback One – Books are time consuming to read and often more general in scope than the focus of your essay. (Give an example.)

Drawback Two – The few books you select to read may share a perspective and neglect to give you a fair view of alternative perspectives. (Give an example.)

Journals

Advantage One – A journal article, being much shorter than a book, will be focused on a more specific aspect of a subject which you select in line with the focus of your essay and thus give your work some depth. (Give an example of an article focused on some aspect of this essay.)

Advantage Two – Because journal articles are more concise, you can read several, giving a variety of views. (Give examples of two articles with different slants on the same subject.)

Drawback One – A journal article, being limited in scope, may neglect or take for granted the context, background and implications of the topic under discussion. (Example.)

Drawback Two – A journal article being concisely written, often for academics, may be hard to understand without prior background reading of introductory books. (Example.)

(Continued)

(Continued)

Conclusion

Give own view – books are the core repository of knowledge but journal articles bring new knowledge to our attention. Also discuss the additional benefit of professional magazines and journals. End with the suggestion that we see a balance of advantages and drawbacks, which suggests that using several sources of information with an awareness of the nature of each will provide depth (e.g. journal articles), breadth (e.g. books) and variety (e.g. mass media, Internet).

Essay Two: The Two Part Essay: *Explain and discuss the four aspects of Brookfield's notion of critical thinking. How well do these aspects, taken as a conception of critical thinking, fit with your own ideas about what it is?*

Before you write your plan for this essay you will have read Brookfield's own work on critical thinking and have identified and read books and articles on critical thinking as well as discussions of Brookfield's ideas by other authors, including by some whose own thinking or teaching have been influenced by Brookfield. You will have made some key notes from this reading. Note the word allowance for the essay, the deadline and the voice (personal or passive) expected.

Note that the essay has two parts and that part one must cover all four aspects of Brookfield's (1987) notion of critical thinking. Now think about the essay title, note that you must both explain and discuss each of the four aspects. (This may mean that part one will require rather more words than part two.) Note that part two is asking a question that requires your opinion and (implicitly, as we will see in Chapter 3) your reasons for this opinion.

Tutor Assessment

For this 3,000–4,000 word essay, the tutor will want to see that you have correctly identified the four aspects and understand what each means. They will want to read some discussion of each. The tutor will also expect that you have addressed part two by developing your own conception of critical thinking and comparing this with Brookfield's.

Chapter 4, the chapter on Critical Thinking, provides an example of this essay. This example is both well planned and critical.

Word Allocation (This is always approximate, provisional and revisable.)

Plan Two

Part One

- You could allocate 500 words to the introduction = 500 words.
- You could allot 500 words for each aspect (include 'explain' and 'discuss') = 2000 words.

Part Two

- You could allocate 500 words for your own conception = 500 words.
- You could allocate 500 words for the comparison with Brookfield = 500 words.
- You could allocate 500 words for the conclusion = 500 words.

Total = 4,000 words.

Sample Plan Two

Explain and discuss the four aspects of Brookfield's notion of critical thinking. How well do these aspects, taken as a conception of critical thinking, fit with your own ideas about what it is?

Plan

Introduction

The importance of critical thinking. Critical thinking, an important element in rational reflection (Brookfield, 1987). Brookfield gives a clear account of his conception of CT (2001) which focuses on the four key aspects discussed in Part A of this essay. (Mention other possible aspects.) Conceptions of critical thinking (Day, 1999; Altiero, 2006).

In Part B, consider own conception of critical thinking and compare with Brookfield's conception.

Part A. Brookfield's Conception

SEC I – Identifying and Challenging Assumptions

Explain (Connect with implicit and hidden assumptions and biases and values)

Discuss

SEC II – Challenging the Importance of Context

Explain

Discuss (Link with cultural diversity (ref))

(Continued)

(Continued)

SEC III – Imagining and Exploring Alternatives

    Explain

    Discuss (Link with creativity (ref))

SEC IV – Developing Reflective Scepticism

    Explain

    Discuss (This often means asking epistemological and conceptual questions (e.g. – How do we know that? What does X mean?)

Part B. A Broader Conception

Develop my own broad conception of critical thinking. Show that a central part of this consists of Brookfield's four aspects, but that there are additional aspects.

Conclusion

Own view. Brookfield's ideas very influential (as shown above).

His four aspects bring clarity to reflection, guard us against biased thinking and help us to form our own point of view, which is, I suggest, another aspect of critical thinking. My own conception is broader and has added additional aspects to those of Brookfield.

Add the final suggestion that which of these many aspects are used will partly depend upon the material about which one is reflecting.

Essay Three: *Evaluate arguments, made by nursing staff, for and against family presence during emergency (medical) situations.*

This 5,000 word essay might be given to nursing students, probably well into their course. There is much to cover in 5,000 words so you will need to be able to pick out and articulate the key arguments associated with key issues.

This essay takes a kind of debate format. You will need to be familiar with the relevant books and articles detailing international studies but must also evaluate this evidence giving the arguments on both sides of the controversy. A good essay will include your own justified point of view.

Some students, as staff or as relative or as patient, may have experience of this issue and drawing on this will enhance the essay provided the tone remains objective, with recognition that the experience could lead you to undervalue one side of the controversy.

Tutor assessment

The tutor will want to see familiarity with and understanding of the relevant, main studies. The tutor will expect you to explain the key issues and to evaluate the main arguments in relation to these.

The debate format of the essay should encourage you to consider arguments and counter arguments. In other words you must show the strengths and weaknesses of the arguments on both sides.

For a good grade the tutor will want to see a well-justified point of view emerging from a consideration of the issues and arguments relating to family presence.

Word allocation (This is always approximate, provisional and revisable.)

Introduction = 500 words
Arguments against = 1,500 words
Arguments in favour = 1,500 words
Evaluating the arguments = 1,000 words
Conclusion = 500 words

Total = 5,000 words.

Sample Plan Three

Evaluate arguments, made by nursing staff, for and against family presence during emergency (medical) situations.

Plan

Introduction

Define emergency medical situations (resuscitation or invasive procedures). Outline of the main international studies (e.g. Fulbrook, 2007; Meyers, 2000).

Brief explanation of the main issues; showing positive and negative staff attitudes to family presence as the key issue.

What follows explores and evaluates staff arguments for and against family presence and concludes that families be allowed to choose unless there are exceptional circumstances.

(Continued)

(Continued)

Staff Arguments Against Family Presence

Staff with less clinical experience of family presence tended to have more concerns including: fear of legal action; concern for the potential negative psychological effects on the relatives' well-being; increased stress for staff.

Staff Arguments for Family Presence

Staff with more clinical experience of family presence tended to have favourable attitude including: family presence can have a positive impact on relatives' psychological well-being; family can be present for the loved one's last words; there is some evidence that being present when a loved one dies helps the grieving process; the patient may derive comfort and support from their family's presence, even when unconscious or an infant.

Evaluation of the Arguments

Emergency medical situations are inherently stressful. It is unsurprising that there are strong arguments on both sides. The arguments about the effects on the family tend to be mirror images of each other, i.e. Some staff argue that the effect will be negative and on the other side, staff argue that the effect will be positive. In reality, impact could vary from family to family. This supports an argument for family choice. Fear of legal action could be countered by arguments about the value of accountability to prevent recurrence of similar tragedies. The other argument against family presence concerns the increased stress on staff, possibly leading to inefficiency. However, it is interesting that staff with more clinical experience of family presence tend to be more in favour. Staff who argue in favour of family presence can point to some very telling benefits. (Last words, the grieving process, the well-being of the patient.)

Conclusion

Because family presence may be beneficial to the family or even to the patient, one could make an ethical case that the decision about presence should be for the family and not for the staff to make. There may be exceptional situations that make family presence unwise. What might these be?...(Guidelines for resuscitation, 2009.)

In addition, although there are strong arguments on both sides, it is significant that staff with more clinical experience tend to be in favour of family presence. Arguably there should be more staff development around this issue and more parent support. On balance (I suggest) the family should be allowed to make an informed decision about their own presence.

Essay Four: The Assessment Type Essay: *How significant is institutional racism in modern Britain?*

This 5,000–6,000 word essay might be given to Sociology students or to students in any of the Social Sciences doing a module on equal opportunities. Though it is framed as a question, it does not require a yes/no answer but a discussion leading to an assessment comprising your own, supported, opinions.

Before you begin, read about ethnic relations and racial disadvantage in Britain, noting material relevant to the significance of institutional racism. Begin to form your assessment about its significance in modern Britain.

Tutor Assessment

For this essay the tutor will want to see that you have read some of the literature about race relations and institutional discrimination in Britain, and have formed a plausible conception of 'institutional racism' and sensible ideas about what would count as 'significant'. They will want to see that you have developed an informed and rational assessment of the significance of institutional racism.

Word Allocation (This is always approximate, provisional and revisable.)

Plan Four

– Introduction = 400 words.
– Analysis of relevant terms and key concepts = 2,000 words.
– Four institutions 800 words each = 3,200 words.
– Conclusion = 400 words.

Total = 6,000 words.

Sample Plan Four

How significant is institutional racism in modern Britain?

Plan

1. Introduction

Point out the need to understand the concept of institutional racism and have some criteria for 'significance'. Outline essay contents. Inclusion of police, education, law, employment as social institutions.

Begin with an analysis 'institutional racism'.

Institutional racism and its significance.

(Continued)

(Continued)

2. Analysis

'Prejudice' 'Discrimination' 'Disadvantage' 'Racism'
    'Institutional Racism' (Make reference to Swann report definition)
    'Significance' – Relate to degree of racial discrimination and disadvantage. (Give some facts and figures over a period of time to explore how equality aims have not been (fully) achieved.)

3. Institutions

- Police (e.g. Stephen Lawrence enquiry).
- Education (Rampton and Swann reports). Qualifications obtained.
- Law – race relations laws. Statistics (Stop and search. Arrests. Sentencing. Imprisonment).
- Employment (Statistics re unemployment, promotions, recruitment practices).

4. Conclusion

Argue that the essay has demonstrated that institutional discrimination is significant in terms of adding to both deliberate and unintentional discrimination to the point of serious racial disadvantage. This biased functioning of our key social institutions is a significant factor in creating racial injustice.

Essay Five. *Discuss how you have made use of each of the following in your studies: The Internet, mass media, journals, books. What do you consider to be the advantages and disadvantages associated with each?*

This is a longer and more self-reflective essay on similar ground to Essay Plan One, but involving metacognition (reflection about one's own learning. This kind of meta-analysis is discussed in the next chapter.)

Tutor Assessment

The tutor will wish to see that in the first part of the assignment the students have discussed all four of the sources identified in the title, relating each to their own studies. How and for what purposes did they use each one? How useful were they in relation to their own learning and in their literature search?

For the second part of the title, the student's discussion of the advantages and disadvantages of each source should demonstrate understanding of the nature of each of these potential sources of knowledge. A good answer will back claims about advantages and disadvantages with good reasons and some of the discussion will link back to their own experiences as discussed in part one of their essay.

Word Allocation (This is always approximate, provisional and revisable.)

Plan Five

- Introduction = 200 words.
- Part One 650 words for each source = 2,600 words.
- Part Two 400 words for each advantage and each disadvantage = 3,200 words.
- Conclusion = 1,000 words.

Total = 7,000 words.

Sample Plan Five

Discuss how you have made use of each of the following in your studies: The Internet, mass media, journals, books.

What do you consider to be the advantages and disadvantages associated with each?

Plan

Introduction – A simple outline of the material to come

Discuss, in turn, my use of the Internet, mass media, journals and books in my studies. Include a brief outline of my studies. Show how and why I selected my material and the use I made of it. Give some indication of how useful I found each source. In the second part of the essay discuss the advantages and disadvantages of each, firstly in my work and secondly, more generally, for teaching, learning and research in my field.

Part One

Internet – Used to check overview of material and references and relevant organisations.
How useful? Discuss shortcuts and caution. Relate to my own learning.

Mass Media – Distinguish between formal and informal learning. Used useful TV documentary and newspaper article. How identified? How useful? Enjoyable! Fresh material. Relate to my own learning.

Journals – Selected key articles (tools used) and the most recent, up to date research. Also benefitted from professional journals. (Details.)

How useful, one particularly focused useful article. Professional sources provided original material.

Make notes of directly relevant material – including title, author, page number. Relate to my own learning.

(Continued)

> *(Continued)*
>
> **Books** – Discuss how the books were selected (book list for course, library, book shop, search tools).
> Discuss checking credibility of author and publisher.
> Read critically – be aware of author background and biases.
> Make notes of directly relevant material – including title, author, chapter, page number.
> Relate to my own learning.
>
> ### Part Two
>
> A)   *Advantages and Disadvantages for my studies*
>
> For each of the sources in turn
>
> B)   *Advantages and Disadvantages in general terms*
>
> For each of the sources in turn
>
> ### Conclusion
>
> There is an overlap of A and B, but there is not a full match – discuss reasons for this.
> All four sources have a role but differences of emphasis for different purposes (examples). Comparisons of each source in relation to my own learning.
> Finally in light of all the above, draw some main conclusions and own view of the advantages and disadvantages of each source. All four sources have both advantages and disadvantages. Allude to these with reference to my own studies discussed in part one. It clearly makes sense to use all four but judiciously.

Negative and Positive Approaches

If you do not plan your essay you may see comments from the assessor such as those below. They point to the common errors made in unplanned essays, including repetition, omission of a section, lack of a logical organisation of your material, an inadequate introduction or lack of a conclusion.

Sample Negative Comments

- Your essay is repetitive.
- You have omitted the second section of the first part of your essay.
- The essay makes some good points but these are given in a random and disorganised way. You need to structure your material.
- You give much less attention to the second part of the essay title.

- Your essay ends somewhat abruptly and without any conclusion.
- Unfortunately your material lacks a clear organisation. It reads as though unplanned.

A well-planned essay will be organised into appropriate sections, with a logical structure within each of these. It will give proportionate attention to all parts of the essay and show links between them. It will open with a good, useful introduction and end with a relevant conclusion. A well-planned essay will receive positive comments such as these:

Sample Positive Comments

- Your essay is well structured.
- Your material is well organised both within each section and in the order of the sections themselves.
- Your sections follow a logical sequence.
- You make clear links between the main, more practical part of the essay, the conceptual analysis in the introduction and the conclusions drawn in the final part.
- Your step by step approach to the topic enabled you to stay in control of complex and interlinked material.

Brief Exercise: Planning Your Essay

Make up an essay question on a topic you know about and construct a practice plan.

Feedback is given in Appendix 4.

Conclusion

Planning your essay will help you to produce a relevant and well-organised piece of work with an appropriate and interesting introduction, well-developed main body and a rounded, relevant and satisfying conclusion. It will have the additional benefits of helping you to stay focused on the essay question and to meet your deadline and word allowance. Planning skills are important because good grades at HE level require well-structured work. Learning how to plan your work helps you to develop a stronger sense of logical structure and good organisation.

Summary of Key Points

It is usually very obvious if an essay has been planned or not. A well-planned essay will be well structured. Its content will be organised in a systematic, sensible way. A plan

(Continued)

(Continued)

helps you to take control of your essay material. What follows is advice on how to construct a brief plan which will help you to produce a good essay.

Write your essay title very accurately at the top of a sheet of A4 paper.

1. Think about what you want to respond and what you have read to explain and support your answer.
2. Next write 'Introduction' and think about what this should include, e.g. define key terms, give background information, set out in brief what your essay will cover.
3. Now consider what should come next and set out your planned answer in brief points organised in a systematic way, section by section.
4. Your final section will be the conclusion. This could sum up the key points of your essay or draw some conclusions on the topic. It needs to round off your essay in a relevant way.
5. Does your plan fit in with the marking criteria and intended learning outcomes for this essay?
6. Use your plan to help you to keep to your word allowance.

To see how to write the brief notes to guide you in each part of your essay, have a look at the sample essay plans provided in this chapter.

For chapter exercise feedback, further reading ideas and more tips on polishing your assignment, check out the appendices at the back of the book.

References

Altiero, J. (2006) *No More Stinking Thinking*. London: Jessica Kingsley.

Brookfield, S. (1987) *Developing Critical Thinkers: Challenging Adults to Explore Alternative Ways of Thinking and Acting*. San Francisco: Jossey-Bass.

Compton, S., Madgy, A., Goldstein, M., Sandhu, J., Dunne, R. and Swor, R. (2006) *Emergency Medical Providers' Experience With Family Presence During Cardiopulmonary Resuscitation*. Aug. 70(2): 22328 Epubl 2006. Jun 27.

Day, C. (1999) *Developing Teachers: The Challenges of Lifelong Learning*. London: Routledge.

Fulbrook, P. (2007) 'Paediatric critical care. Nurses attitudes and experiences of parental presence during cardiopulmonary resuscitation: A European survey', *International Journal of Nursing Studies*, Sept 44 (7): 238–49, Epubl. 2006 Jul (1).

Meyers, T. A., Eichhorn, D.J., Guzzetta, C.E., Clark, A.P., Klein, J.D., Taliaferro, E. and Calvin A. (2000) 'Family presence during invasive procedures and resuscitation: The experience of family members, nurses and physicians', *American Journal of Nursing*. 100(2): 32–43.

The Rampton Report (1981) *West Indian Children in our Schools. Interim Report of the Committee of Inquiry into the Education of Children from Ethnic Minority Groups*. London: HMSO.

The Swann Report (1985) *Education for All. The Report of the Committee of Enquiry into the Education of Children from Ethnic Minority Groups*. London: HMSO.

3

Criticality: Rational Reflection

Reasons, Arguments and Evidence

 Overview

- Introduction
- Higher Education
- Rationality: How to be Rational
- Give Reasons and Arguments
- Provide Evidence
- Sample Essay – Extract from Education for Wolf Conservation
- Avoid Biased Thinking
- Negative and Positive Approaches
- Conclusion
- Summary of Key Points
- References

Introduction

In this chapter we explore what it is to produce rational work and show you how to do this. We explain what it means to be rational and give you the skills to be so; skills of reasoning, argument and the production of sound evidence.

A rational essay gives (good) **reasons** for its claims, produces rational (reasonable) **arguments** for its point of view and, where relevant, refers to reputable research providing **evidence** to back up those claims and point of view. In conjunction with Chapters 4 and 5, this chapter will show you how to write the **reflective** essays appropriate to higher education. Reflective work will contain rational (justificatory) reflection (Chapter 3) critical (questioning) reflection (Chapter 4) and meta (analytic) reflection (Chapter 5). Essays which show elements of these kinds of criticality tend to secure high grades.

We have said that rational reflection involves providing valid reasons, arguments and evidence to back up an essay's contentions. Valid reasons are sensible, plausible, intelligent considerations drawn from experience. Valid arguments conform to the rules of formal logic: they are coherent and non-contradictory. Valid evidence draws on relevant, creditable research. As we will see, what counts as evidence varies in different knowledge domains.

Higher Education

Academics in higher education ask good questions. They are rational, critical and analytic in their own field. Part of their role as university lecturers lies in the pursuit of knowledge – extending their own personal knowledge and understanding, extending their students' knowledge and understanding and, through research, seeking to extend human knowledge, our collective understanding, by asking and attempting to answer good questions. Chapters 3, 4 and 5 will help you to develop the academic skills that will enable you to ask good questions and thus to write essays at a more 'critical' level, thereby securing a higher grade. This is the level of work aimed for and eventually expected in 'higher education'.

Higher education is 'higher' in three senses relevant to your need to produce work at an appropriate level.

1. The Research Element

Having completed primary and secondary education, where we absorb knowledge in various subjects, in higher education we are concerned with the task of gaining new knowledge and deeper understanding in our chosen field(s). HE staff have a research role in addition to their teaching responsibilities. Their research should feed their teaching. HE students must begin to develop research skills which are reflected in their work. You must learn how to find the key literature, how to identify relevant seminal works and relevant new research and, for some assignments, students may need to undertake a small scale research project of their own.

2. Criticality

Students must also develop an academic focus on rationality. You must identify sound evidence and produce logical reasoning for the case you are making. Another aspect of being rational is to learn to be critical. This involves skills such as recognising and challenging assumptions and implicit values, developing a reflective scepticism, categorising complex material, comparing and contrasting ideas, theories, and research findings and forming your own point of view.

3. 'Meta'-Level Thinking

'Meta' means 'above', 'after' or 'beyond'. In HE we need to learn how to think at this meta-level. Meta-thinking is both taking an overview (view from above) and represents a higher (more analytic) level of thinking skill. To be analytic often requires that we move from ground level to meta-level thinking. The ground level is the information and facts and descriptions of people's ideas or research findings. The meta-level is the reflection on the ground level material. Thus analytic thinking is not merely descriptive thinking. It is not simply accepting or presenting information. Rather it requires understanding and interpreting and evaluating this information in order to form your own ideas about what is claimed.

When we use meta-level thinking about our own learning and thinking processes (metacognition) we can improve our thinking, learning and understanding through becoming more aware of our own thinking and thus more able to be critical of it.

Rationality: How to be Rational

Preliminary Definitions

- **Empirical**
  Factual. Scientific. Empirical evidence is based on observation and experiment. This is the kind of research evidence that can back up your essay's claims and arguments.
- **Logical**
  i. A valid thought process, coherent and without contradiction. Watch for and change contradictions in your argument.
  ii. Systematic and well ordered. It is in this sense of logical that your planning must be logical to produce well-organised essays.

- **Epistemology**
  Theory of knowledge. Students will become more aware of the nature of knowledge in the different academic disciplines, especially their own. This is relevant for all students

45

and not just those doing philosophy. One of the values of higher education and an implicit goal of your study and of your essays and assignments is the development of knowledge and understanding.

- **Ontology**
  This is the branch of philosophy concerned with what kind of entities exist. In terms of your essay you will be concerned with certain kinds of entities (e.g. hypotheses, arguments, concepts, ideas, theories) and with some particular things (e.g. particular writers or certain modules or, as in Sample Essay One in Chapter 2, two forms of literature or as in Sample Essay Two, four aspects of critical thinking).

- **Accredited Sources of Knowledge**
  These are the means of achieving genuine knowledge and not merely of holding beliefs on the basis of superstition or guesswork. The two main means, or sources, are, firstly, the (scientific) method of observation and experiment. These observations and experiments are replicable by others, unlike, for example, a delusion. Secondly, logical deductions from valid beliefs give us true propositions (knowledge). Read more about accredited and non-accredited sources of knowledge in Chapter 7.

What do we mean by rational thought and rational argument? To be rational is to have reasons for your actions and judgements. 'Reasons', in this academic context, implicitly assumes that these reasons are valid (i.e. that they have good justifications for those actions and judgements). Such reasons support the actions and judgements. The Chambers Dictionary (1998) defines reason as the ground, support or justification of an act or belief. A reason can only provide support or justification in so far as it is valid, sensible, backed up by sound evidence and/or logical reasoning.

In terms of writing an essay, the claims, arguments and point of view being put forward in the essay are only rational insofar as they are backed up by plausible reasons, sound evidence and logical reasoning. Unsupported claims will be assessed as 'too assertive'. Claims supported by good reasons and arguments and evidence will be seen by the essay assessor as justified, even if they disagree! The point is that academics do disagree among themselves but wherever there are two or more points of view in the field, there are arguments in favour of each view. A rational essay will show awareness of differing viewpoints and their justifications, but when you put forward your own preferred view, you will give reasons for why you prefer it. Show why you think the justifications for it are stronger than the justifications for opposing views. A fair assessor will not be concerned about whether they agree with your view, but whether and how well you have supported it. In order for your essay to be rational you need to understand the characteristics of good reasons and valid arguments and know how to draw on **reputable** research to support your point of view. In short, a rational essay provides reasons for the claims it makes. It will thus justify its own claims and discuss the credibility of the claims of relevant thinkers and writers in the field. As the author of the essay you will thus show that you recognise good empirical evidence and logical argument. Your essay will not be full of unsupported and unjustified claims and assertions.

Give Reasons and Arguments

Without evidence and sound argument we have no reason to prefer one belief or theory to another. We will explore what makes for sound evidence in the next section, but first, we will consider what makes for logical argument.

Logical Sequence

As well as in the context of formal logic, which is discussed below, there is a more everyday sense of 'logical', meaning 'orderly and well structured'. A logical structure in an essay will be one in which the material is organised in a systematic and sensible fashion. For example, one might put the most important points first or arrange arguments from the most simple to the more complex. Similarly you might explain B before A because understanding A requires prior understanding of B. Thus rational essays, as well as providing reasons, evidence and valid deductions will also seek order and systematic structure in their organisation. Planning an essay, as we have considered in Chapter 2, will help your essay to have this kind of well-ordered (logical) structure.

Formal Logic

A logical argument draws valid conclusions from reasonable premises. In other words, logical reasoning proceeds from premises (assumptions) via valid logical deduction to justified conclusion. Such valid conclusions may or may not be true. This depends on the truth (or falsehood) of the premises. Valid logical deduction follows a pattern or structure dictated by the three laws of logic. For example, contradictions in an argument break the first law of logic. It cannot be raining and not raining at the same time in the same place.

Formal logic is a symbolic system with rules for moving from premises to valid conclusions. You do not need to have done a course in formal logic to recognise valid and invalid deductions and consistent and inconsistent statements. We have a grasp from our understanding of language of consistency and contradiction. However, if you would like to know more about formal logic there are several available introductions available.

Jeffrey, R.C. (2006) *Formal Logic: Its Scope and Limits* (4th edition, J.P. Burgess ed.) Indianapolis, IN: Hackett Publishing.

Bowell, T. and Kemp, G. (2005) *Critical Thinking: A Concise Guide* (2nd edition). Abingdon: Routledge. (This useful book contains chapters on deductive and inductive logic. It also covers good and weak argument and critical thinking together with some philosophical reflections on truth, knowledge and belief.)

Here are the basic structures of logical deduction and logical contradiction.

Logical deduction – If A is true then B is true.

A is true.

Therefore B is true.

Logical Contradiction – A is true and A is not true.

A Note on Cause and Effect

A common error is to mistake correlation for cause. An event may correlate with another event without one having been caused by the other. For example, if I get a headache after a fall, an injury from the fall may have caused the headache. This may need to be checked by my doctor. However, the headache could, of course, be coincidental; caused by something other than the fall. Causation cannot be assumed.

Some Examples of Plausible Arguments and Rational Statements

Logical Deduction

If it rains hard for half an hour then the pavements will be wet. It has rained hard for half an hour, therefore the pavements are wet.

Contradiction

A good essay must be well structured. √
This essay is disorganised but it is a good essay. X

Cause Precedes Effect

Because it is raining (cause) she has taken her umbrella (effect). √
She has taken her umbrella (effect) because it is raining (cause). √
It is raining because she has taken her umbrella. X

Assertive and Rational Statements

The following Table 3.1 distinguishes between rational statements and unsupported (assertive) statements.

TABLE 3.1   Assertive and rational statements

Rational (Valid) Statements	Assertive (Unsupported) Statements
The focus on human occupation means that occupational therapy can sometimes be a catalyst for social action and change: by equipping their clients with social and occupational skills, the occupational therapist enables them to be agents who can generate changes in their own lives, in their families and even in the wider society.	The focus on human occupation means that occupational therapy can sometimes be a catalyst for social action and change.
People with physical, mental and cognitive disorders often experience social exclusions of many kinds which means that occupational therapists, in practice, often work with clients who are relatively isolated, having little contact with others.	Occupational therapists, in practice, have concerns for people they think are isolated.
Occupational therapists need group work skills to both work effectively in a team with other health care professionals and to be successful in therapeutic group work with groups of clients.	Occupational therapists need group work skills.
In my experience (having been a tutor for ten years) many students, faced with their first essay, do not know how to get started.	All students, when faced with their first essay, do not know how to get started. (Beware of 'All or Nothing' thinking displayed in words such as 'all' and 'every'. It is unlikely that all students have the same experience when approaching their first essay.)
Some students know how to begin an essay, but many find it difficult to get started.	Students begin their first essay with confidence but the majority do not know how to get started. (This sentence is unclear.)
Some students feel confident about an essay, but when they begin to write, they find it more difficult than they had expected.	Students begin their first essay with confidence but the majority do not know how to get started. (This sentence is ambiguous. It could mean what the clearer sentence opposite states or it could mean what the sentence above the one opposite states.)

Plausible Arguments

A plausible statement is one which, according to our own experience and reasoning, is likely to be valid. We still need supporting evidence to accept it

49

as more than plausible, i.e. as true. An implausible statement, on the other hand, is, as our own experience and reasoning would suggest, dubious in some way. Here are some examples:

- Smith could not have committed the killing because he has an unbreakeable alibi for the time it took place.
- Although Smith's alibi means that he could not have done the killing himself, it is possible that he paid someone else to do it (of course just because an event is possible does not entail that it actually happened).

Implausible Arguments

- Smith must have had no connection with the murder because his alibi is unbreakable.
- Jones has got an A grade for the first time. She must have plagiarised. (Beware of 'all or nothing' words like 'must'. Jones may have worked particularly hard this time, or perhaps has always been interested in this topic, or has recently benefitted from additional tutoring. The suddenly much improved grade may need to be looked into, but no immediate conclusions should be jumped to.)

Provide Evidence

The scientific method is based on observation and experiment (empirical evidence). It proceeds by disproving claims through observation and measurement of phenomena in the world. A hypothesis is always held as true, *provisionally*, since science makes progress through falsification of our hypotheses. Thus, propositions we hold (provisionally) as true are based on experience of the real world of objects and forces existing in time and space. It is a rigorous form of evidence because it must be replicable (testable) by others. (Experiences which we all share or could share are called *intersubjective* as distinct from subjective experiences such as hallucinations, dreams or delusions).

In everyday life we constantly rely on the evidence of our senses (empirical) and on logical reasoning from this experience (reasoned argument). For instance: *James is due now. I can hear a car approaching. It is probably him.*

Most of our reasoning is based on simple arguments incorporating relevant facts. 'Facts' include psychological and sociological and educational 'truths' as well as empirical data.

- This essay is about good practice in teaching. My tutor has written a book and papers about Schön. It would be sensible to consider 'reflection-in-action' as part of good practice.
- My previous essay was marked as 'too assertive'. If I want to get a better grade, I must justify my claims in this one!
- I have written less than half my essay and half the time has gone. I will be in hospital next week. I should see my tutor before then about having a deadline extension.

Identify Relevant and Credible Research (Evidence)

Good evidence for the claims or assertions made in your essay can be found in relevant research, written up in books and papers about the subject of your essay. You need to be able to identify and use such research findings.

Not all information is credible. To identify what is credible as you conduct your research, you will need to evaluate the following:

Authority

- Where was the information published and by which organisation or company? Was it an academic publisher, a government source, self-published or from a more popular source?
- Who is/are the authors? Are they considered experts in their field? Does the evidence appear well researched with appropriate references and citations? Is the author cited in other references (this can give an indication of their authority)?
- What is the source of the content and information? Is it accurate? Is it based on primary or secondary research (primary sources are the raw material from first-hand, empirical research, secondary sources are based on primary sources. You may need to double-check the primary source to establish the credibility and value of the source.)

Purpose

- Evaluate the tone of language and style of the information. Are there any obvious biases? Credible and reliable sources tend to use a more objective approach unless the information is a self-reflective or anecdotal piece. Check the background of the author(s) to assess their experience, current and past job roles, and, where possible, their values and beliefs.
- What is the intention of the author(s)? Is the content fact or opinion? Could it be seen as propaganda? Is the point of view objective and impartial?

Currency and Relevance

- Is the information current and/or topical? As a general rule of thumb, the information should be up to date and published relatively recently, although this is not always the case. We have mentioned Darwin's *The Origin of Species* earlier, and this is an example where it would be relevant to cite and quote from this original source even though it was published in the 1800s.
- Is the information relevant to your research topic? We are bombarded with so much information in the technological age that it can be easy to veer off track. By regularly checking relevancy, you will stay focused and directed on the research question.
- Research that is directly relevant to your essay question gives evidence to back up the claims you are making.

In the following extract from a long (10,000 word essay), the student has drawn on international research. In an essay on education for wolf conservation, she first wanted to establish the different factors contributing to the need for such conservation.

> ### Sample Essay – Extract from Education for Wolf Conservation
>
> Habitat loss and fragmentation through increasing urbanisation and infrastructure development has also seen wolves and many other species pushed into marginal areas which are either protected parks or areas where human habitation is either not feasible or not attractive enough (Boitani, 1995; Sillero-Zubiri, 2005). However, increased wolf numbers, and reduced populations of wild prey, lead to wolves coming into more frequent contact with human populations as they disperse and seek new territories and more suitable habitat (Mech and Boitani, 2003; Woodroffe et al., 2005). This increasing contact can, and often does, lead to varying levels of 'conflict' (Bath, 2009).
>
> *These important background claims are well supported from research evidence.*

Avoid Biased Thinking

It is difficult to be unbiased when our values and emotions are deeply involved in the subject of our thinking. For example, parents are often reluctant to accept that their child misbehaved in an incident at school. All the parents of the children involved are inclined to see their child as being led astray by others. We should be aware of these areas of prejudice and check for hidden assumptions, dubious generalisations and unfairness. Common social prejudices (which lead to discrimination and disadvantage) include: racism, sexism, homophobia, ageism and prejudice against the disabled and the mentally ill. For example, black people aren't musical, girls like cooking, gay people are more likely to be paedophiles, old people are forgetful, disabled people need help, the mentally ill are violent. These are subjects of thinking, judgement and claims in which we need to be particularly careful and self-critical. In the examples given, not all members of the group conform to generalisations about the group. Not all black people are musical, some girls hate cooking, most gay people, like most heterosexuals, are not paedophiles, not all elderly people are forgetful, not all disabled people need help (or no more than do the able-bodied) and not all mentally ill people are violent.

Prejudice is irrational and tends to lead us into biased generalisations and make us resistant to changing our beliefs in the light of contrary evidence. We see a difference between rational, scientific thinking and prejudice. We are not reluctant to change a scientific hypothesis in the light of new evidence. Indeed, as we have seen, science progresses through seeking such contrary evidence. Prejudice, on the other hand, distorts our perception of evidence when it is at odds with our prejudiced beliefs.

Generalisations based on limited experience may be convenient but they may also lead us into biased thinking and false claims.

Negative and Positive Approaches

If you do not support the claims made in your essay with convincing reasons or valid argument or research findings then you will be seen as too assertive and your essay as lacking in rationality. You should develop a point of view but have some justification for it! Do not merely describe what you or a key writer think – produce supportive reasons, or arguments, or evidence. Indeed in a controversy, produce the rationale for both sides but give reasons for thinking that the view you support has the stronger rationale. Avoid contradictions in your own arguments but point out those of your 'opponents'. In these ways you will avoid negative comments such as:

Sample Negative Comments

- Your essay is too assertive. You must produce reasons and evidence for your main claims.
- Your essay is somewhat contradictory. In the first half you appear to argue that employment prospects for young people are improving and in the second part you agree with writers/researchers who are arguing that this is not the case.
- Your produce reasons for your 'side' of the controversy and have been fair in your outline of the opposite view. You could have produced reasons for rejecting this view or shown why it is weaker or less plausible than it appears.

By producing a convincing justification for your claims, you are demonstrating your ability to be rational and you will gather positive comments such as the following:

Sample Positive Comments

- You make out a good case for your point of view and cite credible, supporting, recent research.

- Having shown, in clear exposition, that both sides in this debate have been supported with relevant and plausible arguments, you go on to produce good reasons for preferring side A.
- You have produced a good case for your answer to the essay question and also given convincing reasons for rejecting the main arguments against your position.

Brief Exercise: Practise Giving Reasons

Environmental education should be part of the compulsory curriculum.

Give a reason to support and a reason against this claim. Can you think of counter reasons to each of these?

Feedback is given in Appendix 4.

Conclusion

We have explored, in some detail, how to produce 'rational' essays. You need to support your 'answer' to the essay question with reasons, arguments and by reference to research findings (evidence) recorded in the literature. In this way, you will avoid the charge of being too assertive. You will have used one aspect of the criticality which secures high grades in HE.

Summary of Key Points

In this chapter the focus has been on producing a rational essay. If you wish to achieve a high grade then being rational is important. The following tips will help you to write a rational essay.

1. To be rational means providing valid reasons to back up your claims and ideas. Valid reasons are sensible, plausible, intelligent points drawn from your experience or points put forward by writers with whom you agree. Do not forget to reference these. To be rational also means providing valid arguments in support of your point of view. Valid arguments are coherent – logical and non-contradictory.
    To be rational requires you to write in an orderly and well-structured sequence.
2. To be rational also means citing relevant, creditable research in support of your answer to the essay question. Such research will be found in some of the literature relevant to your essay topic.
3. Not all research is reliable. To evaluate research findings consider where it was published, e.g. reputable academic publisher or popular newspaper? Who was the author? Is it objective or is it propaganda? Does it have a commercial motivation?

4. Are the research findings recent and relevant?
5. Prejudice often leads to biased thinking. Be aware of your own prejudices and those of others, including instances of the endemic social prejudices: racism, sexism, homophobia, ageism, prejudice against the disabled and the mentally ill.
6. Being rational gives a critical edge to your work. This is the critical level aimed for in HE and it will help you to achieve a high grade for your work.
7. There are often two or more points of view about your essay question. It does not matter if your assessor disagrees with your point of view. What he or she expects is that you will show awareness of the different views and their rationales and that you have produced good reasons or arguments or evidence in support of your own view.

Table 3.1 in this chapter gives examples of assertive and rational statements.

For chapter exercise feedback, further reading ideas and more tips on polishing your assignment, check out the appendices at the back of the book.

References

Bath, A.J. (2009) 'Working with people to achieve wolf conservation in Europe and North America', in M. Musiani, L. Boitani and P.C. Paquet (eds), *A New Era for Wolves and People: Wolf Recovery, Human Attitudes, and Policy*. Calgary: University of Calgary Press. pp. 173–200.

Boitani, L. (1995) 'Ecological and cultural diversities in the evolution of wolf–human relationships', in L.N. Carbyn, S.H. Fritts and D.R. Seip (eds), *Ecology and Conservation of Wolves in a Changing World*. Edmonton, Alberta: Canadian Circumpolar Institute. pp. 3–11.

Bowell, T. and Kemp, G. (2005) *Critical Thinking: A Concise Guide* (2nd edition). Abingdon: Routledge. (This useful book contains chapters on deductive logic and on inductive logic. It also covers good and weak argument and critical thinking together with some philosophical reflections on truth, knowledge and belief.)

Jeffrey, R.C. (2006) *Formal Logic: Its Scope and Limits* (4th edition, J.P. Burgess ed.). Indianapolis, IN: Hackett Publishing.

Mech, L.D. and Boitani, L. (2003) 'Grey wolf (Canis lupus)', in C. Sillero-Zubiri, M. Hoffman and D. Macdonald (eds), *Canids: Foxes, Wolves, Jackals and Dogs: Status Survey and Conservation Action Plan*. Gland, Switzerland: IUCN. pp. 124–8.

Sillero-Zubiri, C., Hoffman, M. and McDonald, D (eds) (2005) Canids: Foxes, Worres, Jackals and Dogs. *Status Survey and Conservation Action Plan*. Gland, Switzerland: IUCN.

Woodroffe, R., Thirgood, S. and Rabinowitz, A. (eds) (2005) *People and Wildlife: Conflict or Coexistence?* Cambridge: Cambridge University Press.

4

Criticality: Critical Thinking

Introduction

In the previous chapter we looked at being rational, taking this to mean reason giving, rational arguments (reasoning) and producing evidence for one's claims. It was, essentially, about justification. A good essay does not merely make assertions but justifies these. This is part of the rationality required in HE level work. Another HE requirement is to know how to take a critical approach to the essay question. This is to know how to practise the kind of questioning and the kind of reflection covered in this chapter. We will show you how to ask the right questions and how to reflect meaningfully on the essay question and your answer.

A descriptive piece of work can provide interesting, well-written, well-organised material. However, to lift this material to a 'higher' level requires questioning reflection – what we might call 'critical thinking'.

Critical Thinking

Thinking, including critical thinking, is associated with electrochemical processes that take place in our brain, but our awareness of it is as a mental process taking place in our mind. To understand and use critical thinking in your essay does not involve knowing about brain processes. Rather, critical thinking involves knowing about mental processes – your **conscious** attempts to make sense of your essay material, its key concepts, theories, research data and central issues. To make this material **meaningful** is to enable both you and your reader to better **understand** it. Critical reflection deepens your understanding of your material. Critical reflection uses Brookfield's (1987) aspects of critical thinking, which are discussed later, and by practising the use of these mental acts you will learn to become increasingly and more effectively critical.

The notion of thinking can be subdivided in various ways (see Table 4.1 on positive and negative thinking). For example: scientific thinking, critical thinking, creative thinking and caring thinking and so on. Some of these categorisations overlap. Scientific thinking connects with the concern for evidence touched on in Chapter 3 and creative thinking comes into Brookfield's second 'aspect' of critical thinking. In terms of essay writing, critical thinking **interrogates** the essay question (title) to get clearer about what is being asked and **evaluates** (makes an assessment of) the possible answers. Creative thinking makes new connections. Collaborative thinking builds on group thinking from seminars and builds constructive possible answers. Caring thinking brings commitment and concentration to seeking understanding and appreciates the values dimension of questions.

In non-academic contexts, to be critical often implies pointing out flaws and weaknesses. It is to take a negative stance to something: a book, a building, a person's actions, etc. It can even be 'nitpicking'. However, in the academic sense of 'critical', negativity is not exclusively implied. In critical thinking we explore both the strengths and the weaknesses of an idea, theory, argument or of research data. Indeed, after interrogation and reflection, our overall evaluation may be either favourable or unfavourable, but with a more nuanced appreciation of both positive and negative aspects of the item we have evaluated. Of course, it is fair to say that when we subject material to critical scrutiny, we often expose aspects which are implausible or improvable! Similarly, it is when we subject our own beliefs and ideas to critical scrutiny that we improve, sometimes even transform them.

57

TABLE 4.1   Positive and negative thinking

POSITIVE	NEGATIVE
Scientific thinking	**Irrational thinking**
Evidential	Prejudiced
Logical	Superstitious
Rational	Wishful thinking
Collaborative	Assertive
Critical thinking	**Uncritical thinking**
Rational	Unsupported
Questioning (assumptions, context, alternatives)	Unreflective
Analytic	Unexamined
Sceptical	Accepting
Creative thinking	**Conventional thinking**
Lateral	Linear
Imaginative	Clichéd
Constructs alternatives	Fixed
Careful thinking	**Careless thinking**
Conscientious	Slipshod
Paying attention to detail	Lack of attention to detail
Respect for accuracy	Unconcerned about errors
Caring Thinking	**Uncaring Thinking**
Showing concern and respect for people	No concern or respect
Showing concern and respect for knowledge	Lack of concern for truth
Ethical	Lack of ethical awareness
Collaborative thinking	**Egotistical thinking**
Works with others – collaborative	Ignores the work of others
Constructive – builds on the work of others	Ignorant of the work of others

Interestingly, the Chambers dictionary (1998) defines a 'critic' as someone who assesses something, and 'critical' as relating to a turning point, transition or crisis and also as rigorously discriminating. One element of critical thinking surely it is to seek to make fair and insightful judgements, assessments or evaluations, and another element is surely to ask rigorously discriminating questions. And many theorists, for example Mezirow, see the making of meaning and understanding in terms of a transition in thought, what he calls 'perspective transformation' (Mezirow, 1981). In gaining an understanding or insight we often have the experience of a reorientation of our perspectives, ideas or evaluations.

To sum up, critical thinking refers to those questioning thought processes which help us to better understand our essay material.

In what follows, we explore and demonstrate these thought processes. We begin with the four aspects of critical thinking set out by Brookfield (2001). We begin with these four aspects because they are key ideas which are clear and useful for critical essay writing. In order to be as comprehensive as possible we will also look at some additional ways of thinking which will help you to be critical in your work.

The Tools of Critical Thinking

Brookfield's Four Aspects

1. Identifying and Challenging Assumptions

Assumptions are propositions or claims that we accept without having reasons or evidence for them. We cannot think without some assumptions. For example, this whole chapter is based on the assumption that critical thinking is a good thing and that seeking to better understand material is a worthwhile objective.

Every argument begins with some 'given' (accepted as true) proposition. Critical thinking will seek to be aware of the assumptions that are being made in any claim or argument and will assess if they are acceptable and sound.

Some assumptions may be hidden or indirect and can be spotted and examined. For example, take the statement: *Brookfield has explained what is meant by critical thinking.* An assumption here is that Brookfield has given the definitive account of critical thinking, to be accepted as its essential meaning. Actually, he has provided one account of critical thinking, albeit, when we reflect on it, a useful one for students seeking to produce a good essay.

Some hidden assumptions are the implicit values built into a statement. For example: *the children must have homework if they are to cover the whole syllabus.* The indirect assumption here is that the whole syllabus cannot be covered in school time. A hidden value is that the material in the syllabus, in its entirety, is worth learning (represents worthwhile knowledge).

Some assumptions are acceptable and some are dubious, perhaps based on prejudiced generalisations and stereotypes. The point is that our thinking cannot proceed without taking some propositions for granted – we cannot explore and evaluate every proposition simultaneously. However, to gain clarity and deeper understanding of our essay material, we need to be aware of the assumptions being made in order to test these against our own experience and knowledge. We question that which is being assumed or taken for granted.

To reflect on your essay material about assumptions ask:

- What has been assumed by the essay question?
- What has been assumed in the material I plan to use in response to it?

59

- Are these taken for granted assumptions valid?
- What values are in place in the essay material or in my intended response and do I accept these?
- What rationale supports the assumptions on which my own argument is based? Is it a plausible one? For example, in the essay given as a sample, the essay question assumes that Brookfield's work is worth exploring. The essay itself, the essay answer, assumes that the writer's broader conception has added worthwhile aspects. Given the nature of these aspects, this worthwhileness is plausible, and supportive considerations are included.

2. Challenging the Importance of Context

Similarly, we need to be aware that the essay material is never context free. All ideas are influenced by at least some of the following: history, economic and political background, culture, time and place, environmental influences, values, etc. In developing this awareness of the context of a particular set of ideas, we are better able to understand it and to evaluate it.

In the concrete world of objects we can recognise that the same object will look tiny in a large room and disproportionately huge in a small one. Similarly, in the more abstract world of ideas, we need to take context into account. We need to develop a grasp of relationships – the relationship between an object or an idea and its surroundings. Some would argue that this ability to think relativistically is an important intellectual skill, which represents a higher intellectual stage. As a meta-level skill it could also be seen as a form of analytic skill, the skills discussed in the next chapter.

Even for the keywords in an essay question, their context may repay consideration. We have all experienced how words can be twisted when taken out of context by gossips or politicians. Words are influenced by context. They take their meaning from how they are being used in a particular situation. They take on different nuances in different contexts.

To reflect on your essay material about context ask:

- What background factors are influential for this essay question?
- Which of these factors need to be taken account of?
- Which background factors should I discuss in my essay and how much space should I allot to this?
- What do I bring to the question or to my response from my own background, my values and my emotions?
- What are the important contextual factors for this particular part of my essay? Thus, in Chapter 2, the first sample essay on 'sources of information for essay work', the Internet is included. In a modern context, the Internet has become too widely used as a source of information not to be included.

60

3. Imagining and Exploring Alternatives

Adopting a different perspective and exploring other possible points of view enables us to think beyond the obvious and the given. Thinking up an alternative encourages lateral thinking, imagination and creativity. This often brings a fresh, original dimension to our work. Thinking of alternatives also provides the opportunity for comparing and contrasting the material under reflection with alternative material, and thus we become more aware of its strengths and weaknesses. We also become aware that this material is not the only possible way of thinking.

The difference that changing a point of view can make is well illustrated in nature films. When the film adopts the lion's point of view, we hope that she soon catches prey to feed her young. When it adopts the impala's point of view, we hope that the fleeing creature manages to escape.

To imagine and explore alternatives in your essay material ask:

- What other ways could I look at this essay question and at the material in my essay?
- How many alternative perspectives can I think of and are they all are equally reasonable or useful?
- Are there other possible meanings or explanations?
- Is there another plausible interpretation of this essay question, these ideas or this research data? Thus, for example, an essay question about the mind will be interpreted differently by someone who sees a question about the mind as reducible to a question about the brain – not conceptualising the mind as a separate entity from the physical brain. Similarly, in a recent TV documentary, research data was interpreted as establishing a dog's ability to understand human emotions. The same data could have been explained/interpreted in terms of Pavlov's conditioning (see Pavlov, 1927).

4. Developing Reflective Scepticism

Because an 'authority' makes a claim, it is not necessarily true. Because a belief has always been accepted, does not necessarily make it true. Because something has always been done that way, it does not mean it is necessarily the best or only way. We should question claims to universal truth and claims to being the best or only way of thinking or acting. To develop an habitually questioning attitude will often bring out dubious assumptions and values and identify incomplete or culturally relative claims.

Exploring your essay material with reflective scepticism ask:

- Have I understood the essay question correctly?
- Have I interpreted and explained the key writers accurately?
- Have I been sufficiently critical of the ideas, theories and writers?

- Are the reasons, arguments, rationale, given by myself or others valid, consistent, convincing? For example, creationists argue that we know from the Bible that God created the world in seven days. However, this thesis is not consistent with scientific knowledge and the argument from the Bible is not convincing. The Bible deals in metaphor and parable.

These four approaches to your essay material help you to be critical and thus they help you to understand that material more clearly. When you question and reflect on its assumptions and context, and consider alternatives and take a sceptical stance towards its claims you bring that critical edge to your thinking which is required to achieve a good grade.

Aspects of Critical Thinking Additional to Brookfield's

Form Your Own Point of View

In responding to an essay question, you are developing your own point of view about it. To do so critically is not just to stick to what you have always believed, or to unquestioningly accept your tutor's view or the perspective of your key text. It is to seek to arrive at your own opinions in the light of your own experience and in the light of the reasons and evidence you have and in the light of the questions and reflections you have engaged with. Christopher Day, in *Developing Teachers: The Challenges of Lifelong Learning*, puts it thus: 'When we think critically, we come to our judgements, choices and decisions for ourselves, instead of letting others do this on our behalf.' (Day, 1999: 32).

In forming your own point of view, you adopt reflective scepticism to ask questions, to notice assumptions, to take account of context and to imagine alternatives. You evaluate the evidence. Is it sound, reliable, plausible? You hold your point of view provisionally, on the basis of the evidence to date. You assess the evidence against your own experience and the research and arguments of reputable thinkers. You will notice cultural bias or any 'stinking thinking' (Altiero, 2006).

Essay questions require you to develop your point of view in your response. You often need to show awareness of other points of view and your own point of view about these!

Avoid Stinking Thinking (Altiero)

Sometimes critical thinking is defined by what it is not. Examples of thinking that is not critical include: irrational thinking (e.g. superstition), unjustified thinking (e.g. sweeping unsupported claims), biased thinking (e.g. infected with endemic social prejudices), contradictory argument and uncritical reproduction of the ideas of others. Check out your ideas, arguments and claims to detect and eliminate stinking thinking. For example, have you reproduced ideas drawn from the literature uncritically, are your arguments and assumptions in part one of your essay consistent with those in part two, and have your claims gone beyond their support – perhaps by claiming 'all' instead of 'some'?

Engage in Reflective Practice

We can also practise reflection when we are engaged in the practice of a skill such as teaching or indeed such as writing an essay. In his influential work, Schön (1983) has called this 'reflective practice'. A reflective practitioner thinks critically about his or her practice (teaching or writing etc.) before, during and after the activity.

Reflection Before Your Essay

Before writing your essay you think about the title, you do some reading and note making and you make a plan.

Reflection-in-Action

Active reflection while you are actively engaged in writing your essay means that you will not only be critical while you are preparing your essay, but that you will also be critical during the writing process itself. This reflection-in-action will have immediate influence on your writing as you are working.

Reflection After Writing

And, of course, after the writing, you look back to reflect on what you have written. This reflexive criticality enables you to improve your work. Seek to be a reflexive as well as a reflective writer, taking a critical stance before, *during* and after the construction of your essay.

Find a Critical Friend

If you ask a trusted person to read a draft of your essay, invite them to be critical. Do not take offence at their comments as they are seeking to help you, but think critically about their suggestions, making your own mind up about these. Some students develop a critical friendship. This is a voluntary partnership of equals, to provide support and critical feedback on each other's work. This will help you both to become more reflective about your written work and thus to produce better essays.

Classify, Compare and Contrast

Explore your material in order to make classifications and to make comparisons and show contrasts between different parts of it. Sometimes you might make comparisons with other material external to yours. This may enable you to make new links. And, of course, notice and deal with any contradictions you may find. These thought processes are forms of analysis (meta-level criticality) which we will explore in the next chapter.

Top Tip

Question (interrogate) and reflect on your essay question and on your own claims and on the claims of others until a critical approach becomes habitual.

Going Wrong: Insufficiently Critical and Disorganised

Lack of a plan shows in uncritical, disorganised and incomplete essays.

Mal has marked some 50 essays written to this title (*Explain and discuss the Four Aspects of Brookfield's Notion of Critical Thinking. How well do these aspects, taken as a conception of critical thinking, fit with your own ideas about what it is?*). It was obvious which ones were not written to a plan, and – although the subject matter was critical thinking – many were insufficiently critical. Some students reproduced Brookfield's words (e.g. 'identify and challenge assumptions'), but did not explain what this meant in their own words. Several students missed one of the eight elements in the first part of the question ('Explain and discuss the four aspects' asks for eight parts to your answer). Sometimes explanation only was given. Sometimes discussion only. Sometimes one aspect was merged with another. You need eight clearly set out separate elements – explaining and discussing each of four aspects. (See Essay Plan Two in Chapter 2.)

Many students failed to pay proper attention to the second part of the essay question about your own ideas in relation to Brookfield's. Some simply stated that they agreed with Brookfield, but without supporting this. Some would suggest a different conception of critical thinking from that of Brookfield but without giving reasons in support of this conception and without any comparison to Brookfield.

The sample essay which follows is not the only possible good answer to the essay question, but it provides one example of a well-planned, critical piece of work which responds to all parts of the question. Unsurprisingly, the material used in the essay overlaps much of the material explored in this chapter and will, therefore, appear rather repetitive.

Sample Essay: *Explain and discuss the four aspects of Brookfield's notion of critical thinking. How well do these aspects, taken as a conception of critical thinking, fit with your own ideas about what it is?*

Introduction

Critical thinking plays an important part in the academic pursuit of knowledge and understanding. Brookfield's four aspects, as we will see, are essential ways of clarifying, deepening and increasing our understanding of any material which we wish or need to understand. His ideas have been influential, particularly in adult education (Brookfield, 1986.) His numerous books about adult education have included a good proportion on critical thinking because Brookfield believes that a central principle of effective practice in facilitating adult learning is that of critical reflection. (Ibid)

Good first sentences, succinctly giving a conception of critical thinking.

Critical thinking can be distinguished from other important positive forms of thinking, such as creative thinking or scientific thinking. Creative thinking is, arguably, relatively less analytic and more lateral and imaginative than critical thinking, though, as we will see, it overlaps with the third of Brookfield's aspects. Scientific thinking, concerned with empirical evidence, overlaps with the rational questioning which is part of my own conception of critical thinking. Thus we see overlap and connection as well as distinctions between positive forms of thought.

Good point.

However, critical thinking can be more sharply distinguished from irrational, negative thinking or the wishful, biased and contradictory 'stinking thinking' discussed by Altiero (2006). An example of irrational thinking would be thinking based on superstition; an example of biased thinking would be thinking guided by prejudice.

Useful distinctions given.

In the first part of this essay, I explore Brookfield's conception of critical thinking by identifying, explaining and discussing the four aspects of critical thinking identified by Brookfield himself. In the second part I explain, discuss and justify my own conception and show its overlaps and differences with Brookfield's. Brookfield's aspects are a central part of my own conception, and, I will suggest, of

A useful outline of the material to come.

(Continued)

(Continued)

any useful and convincing conception. However, I will argue that my own conception is more comprehensive.

A. Brookfield's Four Aspects

1 Identifying and Challenging Assumptions

What does this mean?

The first of Brookfield's aspects of critical thinking is that of identifying and challenging assumptions. By this he means assumption recognition and analysis. [2001] In other words, Brookfield is suggesting that we should habitually notice and question the assumptions that are being made in the material or the activities under consideration.

Clear explanation. ✓

Assumptions are propositions that we accept without having reasons or evidence for them. Of course, we cannot think without making some assumptions. Every argument begins with some given (accepted as true) proposition.

Useful.

We need to be aware that there are various kinds of assumptions and that some are more dubious than others (e.g. stereotypes). Notice the dubious assumptions in: 'the black boys can go in the running group.' (An assumption about all black boys being good at running.) 'the girls can go in the dance group.' (Assumption about all girls liking to dance.) 'I have wished for a pony for so long that I am bound to get one.' (Assumption that thinking makes it so. This is wishful thinking.) 'I'm so unlucky that something bad is bound to happen.' (Irrational assumption about the efficacy of so-called 'bad luck'.) We need to recognise an assumption in order to test it against our own experience and knowledge. We question that which is being assumed or taken for granted.

Good examples given.

Good point.

Some assumptions may be hidden or indirect but we can learn to recognise and examine these. For example, 'He must have done it as he had means, motive and opportunity.' (The hidden assumption is that means, motive and opportunity are absolute evidence rather than circumstantial.)

✓

Some assumptions are in the form of the values which are implicit in a statement. For example: 'Education has transformed him.' (The assumption of education as worthwhile builds a positive value into the transformation.)

✓

✓

Some assumptions are what Brookfield calls framework assumptions. These are those fundamental assumptions that provide the beliefs upon which our thinking is grounded. E.g.: 'if I dropped this pen it would fall.' (The framework assumption of the law of gravity.)

Good discussion.

Why is identifying and challenging assumptions useful or important?

In his writings about adult education, Brookfield has placed much emphasis on criticality and the identification and the checking of dubious assumptions and of the assumptions that frame our thinking. We cannot be exploring and evaluating every assumption simultaneously. However, to have rational beliefs, we do need to be sure that our framing assumptions, our premises, our implicit values and our hidden/indirect assumptions are reasonable.

√

Indeed, given that to be critical is to be questioning and reflective, to be aware of the basic premises of an argument or to be aware of the implicit or hidden assumptions in a theory or claim seems to be a good starting point for one's questions and reflections about the argument, the theory or claim. One could even argue that not only is this a good starting point, but that without the deeper understanding that awareness of the assumptions being made provides, it would be difficult, arguably impossible, to have a complete grasp of the material under consideration.

2 Challenging the Importance of Context

What does this mean?

Brookfield's second aspect of critical thinking is challenging the importance of context. This means that we should recognise and evaluate the importance of the background of material. In other words, we need to be aware that no claim, theory, argument or data is ever context free. All ideas and practices are influenced by at least some of the following: history, economics, politics, culture, values, time and place and environmental influences etc. In developing this awareness of the context of a particular set of ideas we are better able to understand these and to evaluate them. Thus, for example, when we understand that Dar-

Clear explanation.

√

(Continued)

(Continued)

win developed his great ideas about evolution at a time when it was regarded as heresy to question God's creation of all creatures, we can appreciate his reluctance to publish them. When we appreciate the historical roots of racism, we can better appreciate how irrational and inhumane prejudice became entrenched.

Why is this understanding of context important or useful? To understand the context of material enriches our understanding of it. By placing it in its background we can see its link to a whole network of ideas and gain insight into the historical, social, cultural and religious influences upon it. We may also, in many cases, see the partisan nature of an idea or the power faction it serves. Moreover, by understanding context (cultural context for example) we are more able to imagine alternatives as advocated in aspect three.

Interesting discussion.

When we understand how culture influences our thinking then we are better able to understand why there are variations in beliefs, ways of life and preferences. This in turn will enable us to see that there is no inherent superiority of, say, one style of dress over another and that in more important spheres – value judgements, religious convictions, etc. – we should seek to respect other views. We can begin to understand that we, too, are influenced by our cultural background, a culture which does not unfailingly embody the best or the only acceptable values, customs and practices etc.

These are very good points.

3 Imagining and Exploring Alternatives

What does this mean?

Brookfield's third aspect of critical thinking is 'imagining and exploring alternatives'. This means that we should be thinking up and questioning possible alternative points of view, theories or arguments. In other words, we adopt a different perspective and explore this other possible point of view. This enables us to think beyond the obvious. Thinking of other possibilities encourages lateral thinking, imagination and creativity.

Clear explanation.

Thinking of alternatives also provides the opportunity for comparing and contrasting the material under reflection with alternative material in order to become more aware of its strengths and weaknesses.

An alternative can sometimes take the form of an amalgam of one's own material and other material. For example, at a recent wedding, a Scottish girl was marrying an Egyptian boy. Their mothers developed a menu, for the wedding dinner which fused Scottish and Egyptian cuisine. The result was an interesting, tasty and unusual feast which we all enjoyed.

An original and valid example.

Why is imagining and exploring alternatives important or useful?

Lack of awareness that there are or could be alternative ways of thinking to the one under consideration leaves us vulnerable to the assumption that there is only one way of thinking about something. A claim may be seen as universal or indisputable when it is only one possible claim among several.

Big advances in human knowledge and understanding can come from this ability to imagine alternatives – think of Einstein's new conception of time in his theory of relativity or Darwin's ideas as an alternative to creationism.

✓

The ability to imagine alternatives is not only an aspect of critical thinking, but it is also part of what we mean by 'creative thinking'. Creative thinking, as thinking with the power to create new ideas, relates to this aspect of critical thinking. Both use the imagination, which can produce an element of originality in our thought.

An interesting link.

To learn to imagine alternatives adds to our interrogation of and reflection about ideas and may enable us to see them in a new light with a more nuanced understanding. It sometimes brings a new insight, fresh perspective, exciting amalgam or an original idea. This alternative material may even be better than the original. For example, if you think of a number of alternative conclusions to your essay, one of these may be an equally appropriate but more original conclusion than the one you first thought of.

A good conclusion to your discussion of the third aspect.

(Continued)

69

(Continued)

4 Developing Reflective Scepticism

What does this mean?

Brookfield's fourth aspect of critical thinking is 'developing reflective scepticism'. This means that we should develop an habitually questioning attitude. Because an authority makes a claim does not necessarily mean that it is true. Because a belief has always been accepted does not make it true. Because something has always been done a particular way does not mean it is necessarily the best or only way. Developing reflective scepticism means we should question claims to universal truth and claims to being the best or only way of thinking or acting.

Clear explanation.

√

Why is developing reflective scepticism important or useful?

Brookfield's fourth aspect of critical thinking is not so much a technique for questioning material – like the technique of focusing on and questioning assumptions or the technique of focusing on and therefore recognising important aspects of the context or the technique of imagining alternatives and using these to test material. Rather it is an attitude of mind, attained through the practice of questioning until it becomes an habitual approach. It is to have a critical mind set. This approach prevents my unthinking acceptance of initially plausible and persuasive claims.

Bringing a reflective scepticism to the material will also encourage us to engage with the first three aspects. An habitually questioning attitude will help us to recognise assumptions and to challenge dubious ones. It will help us to recognise the important aspects of context and thus to identify biased, or incomplete or culturally influenced claims. It will help us to see that the claim is not the only possible one, that there are alternative points of view.

An insightful distinction.

Taken together, Brookfield's four aspects of critical thinking will help us to understand ideas. They encourage us to question and reflect on our material. By habitually questioning and reflecting on assumptions, context and alternatives to the material we are presented with, we will sharpen, deepen and enrich our understanding of it. These four

√

√

aspects, therefore, are surely part of what we mean by 'critical thinking'. However, I will suggest, in what follows, that they are not the whole of thinking which is critical.

B. Additional Aspects

In my opinion, critical thinking seeks to interrogate that which is being thought about in order to better understand it, and sometimes to make an assessment of it. By inter- *An acceptable* rogate, I mean 'to bring a searching reflection to bear on *conception.* it'. By bringing a searching reflection to Brookfield's aspects of critical thinking I am able to assess them as useful and important. Mine is a broad conception of critical thinking, since it allows the use of all thinking techniques which can be used in such a searching reflection. √

'Searching reflection' can include what one might call 'rational reflection' – questions concerning the justificatory grounds of what is being thought about. Is it supported by good reasons, valid arguments and evidence? Are its knowledge claims, explicit or implicit, based on valid sources of knowledge? Are my own opinions based on good reasons and evidence? √

A broad conception of critical thinking will also include analytic reflection – analysis which takes an overview of that which is being thought about. Such analysis could include conceptual analysis of key concepts for greater clarity and √ understanding of those concepts. In this essay, it is through some conceptual analysis of critical thinking at the outset, that I am better able to suggest additional aspects of it. Analysis could also include categorisation to bring order and organisation to material. There will always be more than one way of organising material. I have organised the skills of analysis as part of critical thinking. That Brookfield has not included aspects of analysis alongside his four aspects does not imply that he regards skills of analysis as unimportant.

Of course a searching reflection will also include ques- tioning reflection since to interrogate implies a questioning reflection of the kind explicated by Brookfield. Such a ques- tioning reflection, encouraged by reflective scepticism, will √ question the assumptions, context and alternatives to the object of thought under consideration.

(Continued)

(Continued)

In undertaking this critical cognitive journey, the thinker will be better placed to arrive at their own informed and thoughtful point of view. To develop this informed and thoughtful point of view could also be seen as an aspect, or an outcome, of critical thinking. Simply plumping for any point of view is not rational. To be rational, one develops one's point of view as a result of searching reflection on the matter in hand. The more one practises searching reflection, the better one will be at assessing one's evidence and at assessing how provisionally, or how confidently, a point of view deserves to be held. To hold one's point of view provisionally is not being indecisive. It is rational to recognise that we have different degrees and kinds of evidence for our different beliefs and that any one of them may be mistaken.

Good points.

I would suggest that Brookfield's four aspects of critical thinking cover the questioning reflection we need in any comprehensive searching reflection. In other words, these four aspects are surely essential aspects of critical thinking. However, I have suggested other aspects of searching reflection, involved in both rational reflection and meta-reflection, which can also be seen as aspects of critical thinking because they add to our understanding of material through interrogation of it. Through rational reflection we will ask what the justification is for the ideas under interrogation. We can thus evaluate how warranted the ideas are. Through meta-reflection we can analyse the key concepts involved in material. We can also categorise complex material and make comparisons with other ideas in order to better understand those under consideration. I have further suggested that when we try to work out our own point of view about something, we are engaged in critical thinking.

Good point.

Finally, I would add, as a significant example of critical thinking, the ideas of Schön about reflective practice. Schön argues that we can improve our practice, our teaching for example, by reflecting on it before it takes place, during our performance and after it (Schön, 1983). The reflective teacher will think critically when planning their teaching session. In addition, reflecting while actively engaged in teaching has a critical function and an immediate impact on that teaching. Reflecting after the teaching on that teaching means seeking for ways of improving practice in

Good link to reflective practice.

subsequent teaching. By taking a critical stance at all three stages of practice we become better practitioners.

If critical thinking is thought of as a toolbox of skills which enable us to think more deeply and clearly about what we believe or what we should do or are doing, then critical thinking will help us to make more valid judgements and decisions. Using this analogy of thinking skills with tools in the toolbox, one could say that Brookfield has identified and explained the purpose and usefulness of four very important tools, but that there are other useful tools, that could be added to the box!

A useful analogy.

Conclusion

To conclude, Brookfield's ideas fit with my own ideas about critical thinking in the sense that his four aspects of critical thinking are an important part of my own conception. However, I have suggested that there are other aspects and other approaches to a critical interrogation of material which are also useful to further our understanding of it. My own conception of critical thinking is thus a broader one.

A clear summary of your response to the essay question.

Finally, I would suggest that, if we have a full complement of tools in our critical toolbox, which ones we select at a particular point will partly depend on that which we seek to understand. If we wish to gain clarity about a key concept we will use conceptual analysis. If we wish to evaluate data we will consider the validity of the research methods etc. to assess the rational justification for that data. And our understanding of complex or many-stranded material will often be improved by calling on a range of critical thinking skills, those so well identified by Brookfield and the additional ones discussed in this essay.
(2,898 Words)

An original and convincing suggestion.

Negative and Positive Approaches

You have learned from this chapter what we mean by 'critical thinking'. You have learned some questions to ask to identify and challenge assumptions, to recognise the importance of context and to imagine alternatives. You understand the usefulness of developing a healthy scepticism and of being a reflective practitioner. Without such critical questioning feedback on your essay will include comments such as:

Sample Negative Comments

- Your essay provides clear and relevant information but lacks critical edge.
- Too descriptive.
- To take your essay to another level you could have provided critical assessment of the three models which you describe.
- You gave a clear account of two opposite answers to the question posed. But what do *you* think and why?

Through critical questioning you will show understanding of your material; its strengths and weaknesses, its biases and possible alternatives to it. And through this critical understanding you will be able to develop your own well-supported point of view and receive positive comments such as:

Sample Positive Comments

- You demonstrate your understanding of the theory under consideration by correctly identifying its main strengths and weaknesses.
- By challenging the implicit assumptions of the standard point of view you demonstrate the cultural bias it contains. This provides a critical edge to your work.
- You explore alternative perspectives. This allows you to demonstrate critical reflection of a high order.
- You raise some interesting questions and, finally, develop and support your own point of view.

Brief Exercise: Think About Critical Thinking

Answer the following questions:

- Name thinking which is not critical.
- Name Brookfield's four aspects of critical thinking.
- What is the purpose of critical thinking?
- How can critical thinking help you to write a better essay?

Feedback can be found in Appendix 4.

Conclusion

In this chapter we have explored a second aspect of criticality – critical thinking. We have explained the various aspects of critical thinking and in connection with these we have shown you the questions you can ask about your own material and that of others. If you adopt a mindset of reflective scepticism you can then bring the appropriate aspects of critical thinking into play. Some theories will benefit from a consideration of the historical context, some arguments can be criticised by exposing their assumptions, etc. The point is you now have a tool box of critical thinking skills and can select and use each tool as appropriate to the matter under discussion. Using some questioning reflection you will add that critical edge to your essay or assignment which will secure it a better grade.

Summary of Key Points

1. To achieve a high grade for your essay or assignment you need to take a critical approach to the essay question and to your answer. To do this you need to practise critical questioning and reflection on this material. This is what we mean by critical thinking.
2. Such thinking seeks to improve our understanding and will therefore increase your understanding of your essay material.
3. The following four aspects of critical thinking will help your essay to have a critical edge:

    -   Identify assumptions and reflect on these. In other words, what assumptions are being made by the essay question and by your answer to it? What assumptions are being made by the writers you are using? On reflection, are these assumptions reasonable?
    -   What is the context for this essay? What background factors are relevant to the essay question and to your answer? Take account of these.
    -   Imagine alternatives. Sometimes imagining an alternative answer or theory or idea, in addition to showing your understanding of the accepted or traditional ones, will add interest or depth or an element of originality to your answer.
    -   Reflective scepticism. Develop a questioning approach to your work and this will increase your criticality.

4. Reflect on your essay question before you begin your plan and continue to reflect during the planning and during the actual writing. Continue to be critically reflective when you review what you have written.
5. We should avoid stinking thinking – such as superstition, prejudice, wishful bias or unsupported claims.
6. Use aspects of critical thinking as part of developing your own clear and reasonable point of view.
7. Having a 'critical friend' can help you to improve your essay.

For chapter exercise feedback, further reading ideas and more tips on polishing your assignment, check out the appendices at the back of the book.

References

Altiero, J. (2006) *No More Stinking Thinking.* London: Jessica Kingsley.

Brookfield, S. (1986) *Understanding and Facilitating Adult Learning.* Milton Keynes: Open University Press.

Brookfield, S. (1987) *Developing Critical Thinkers: Challenging Adults to Explore Alternative Ways of Thinking and Acting.* San Francisco: Jossey-Bass.

Brookfield, S. (2001) 'Four critical thinking processes'; in B. Raingruber and A. Haffer (eds), *Using Your Head to Land on Your Feet: A Beginning Nurses' Guide to Critical Thinking.* Philadelphia: F.A. Davis. Available from: www.shastacollege.edu/Student%20Services/ Dean%20of%20Students/Health%20%20Wellness/PDF/Stephen%20Brookfield_s %20Critical%20Thinking%20Model.pdf.

Day, C. (1999) *Developing Teachers: The Challenges of Lifelong Learning.* London: Routledge/ Falmer Press.

Mezirow, J. (1981) 'A critical theory of adult learning and education', *Adult Education Quarterly,* 32 (1): 3–27.

Pavlov, I.P. (1927) *Conditioned Reflexes: An Investigation of the Physiological Activity of the Cerebral Cortex* (trans. G.V. Anrep). London: Oxford University Press.

Schön, D. (1983) *The Reflective Practitioner. How Professionals Think in Action.* New York: Basic Books.

5

Criticality: Analytic Thinking

Introduction – Skills of Analysis

In this chapter, as part of the criticality which helps your essay to achieve a higher grade, we will explore four forms of analysis: conceptual analysis; analytic philosophy; meta-analysis – the second level organisation of your first level material, including comparing and contrasting, internal and external links, and evaluation; and metacognition. Each of these forms of analysis will be explained, examples will be given and you will see how analysis can be useful to your essay work, and you will begin to develop analytic skills.

Many students are nervous about words like analysis. To analyse some-thing sounds difficult and complex. Don't allow the thought that you might be asked to analyse something to dent your self-confidence. Once you understand that analysis simply requires you to take an overview of material you will find it begins to make sense. By the end of the chapter you will have acquired a few more critical tools. This time the tools are to use on material of which you are taking an overview. You overview your material in order to organise it, or to see connections, or to recognise its strengths and weaknesses, or to notice differences between different parts of it, etc. Think of analysis as looking over your material in order to see more things about it. Rather like you can see more about a terrain when you have a map which takes an overview of it.

We now turn to the four ways of taking an overview:

- Conceptual Analysis
- Analytic Philosophy
- Meta-Analysis
- Metacognition

One: Conceptual Analysis

Please note that it is customary in academic work to use quotation marks to show that we are talking about a concept. These quotation marks are not used if we have already used the word concept in the sentence. For example:

> We will now explore the concept of education.

> We will now explore 'education'.

Concepts are ideas, not in the sense of mental images or pictures, but in the sense of the mental categories by which we make sense of our experiences of the world. We have concepts of concrete objects, which we can sense [touch and see and hear and smell], such as table, chair, sea, sky, smoke, etc. You can sense the concrete object e.g. a chair, but not the concept of the object, e.g. 'chair'. Our concept of 'chair' is our idea of an object-which-is-for-sitting-on. You cannot sit on the concept itself.

We also have abstract concepts which are not of concrete objects but are abstract ideas such as truth, love, history and education. (You can see the thing, education, going on in classrooms, but you cannot see the concept of education, which is our idea, our mental category, of the kinds of activity which we would count as educational. (e.g. involve worthwhile learning, etc.).

It is abstract concepts which we tend to analyse in our essays in order to become clearer about what they mean – what key distinctions they draw and what characteristics they delineate. It is the abstract concepts which figure in essay questions and which therefore may require some explanation if the essay is to be clear and meaningful to the reader. Think of concepts like education, lifelong learning, professional development, occupational therapy, racism, social psychology, criminality, the subconscious, social class, mental illness, quality, creativity and critical thinking.

When we think about the meaning of an abstract word we are thinking about the concept rather than about the thing itself. To analyse this meaning is to explore the use of the term in a variety of contexts, seeking to understand the distinctions it makes and its defining characteristics. By thus thinking about a complex, abstract term (an idea or concept) we take a meta-level (overview) of its uses and of the necessary and sufficient conditions or criteria for its use, and of what it includes and excludes. Therefore, when in the previous chapter we analysed the concept of critical thinking, we set out its central feature (searching reflection); its main characteristics (identifying and challenging assumptions, etc.); and its overlaps and differences with other forms of thinking, e.g. creative thinking and differentiated thinking which is not critical (e.g. superstitious, prejudiced, etc.).

Many essays benefit from some degree of clarification of the key term or terms central to it. For some essays it will be sufficient to write:

'X is defined as... (......Chambers 1998) and X is used in this way in this essay.'

For other essays, the key terms in the question will need more unpacking than is given by a simple definition. Some words vary in their meaning in different contexts. They are fluid and chameleon. There may be criss-crossing family resemblances (Wittgenstein, 1953: sec 66) between different uses of the term. It may be necessary to explore these different meanings/conceptions with some examples, and to say which conception is relevant for the essay and why.

A minority of essays will be conceptual in their essential nature and will require essay length conceptual analysis!

Use Conceptual Analysis in Your Essay

If your essay is essentially a conceptual one, you will need to produce some sustained conceptual analysis. For example:

*What do you understand by the term **professional development**? What are the educational implications of your answer?*

Note that you are explicitly asked for your analysis of professional development, but that you may also need to give some attention to the concept of education in order to work out the *educational implications* of your analysis.

Other essays may not be so directly conceptual, but would clearly benefit from some analysis. For example:

Write about three forms of in-service professional development of teachers.

You may choose to focus on:

1. Day courses and conferences.
2. Being a reflective practitioner.
3. Personal development as professional development.

In the introduction you can say what you understand by 'professional development', bringing out that you are against a front-loaded conception that excludes development beyond initial training. This will add clarity and depth to your discussion of the three chosen forms of professional development.

A third essay may simply require a relatively brief few sentences saying what, for the purpose of your essay, you are meaning by a key but contested term. For example:

Suggest three important characteristics of a community school

You will need to say what you take a community school to be. This can be in a relatively brief introduction as your main focus will be the three characteristics. However, these characteristics must fit with your idea of a community school.

Sample Essay: *A brief conceptual analysis of professional development*

The concept of professional development brings together two concepts, *profession* and *develop*, which are not only compatible but have a logical link. A profession is a non-manual occupation whose practice requires the possession of complex skills. 'Profession' therefore, implies that professionals have *developed* complex skills. Moreover, a profession is not only a collective body whose members are highly skilled, but the concept also suggest that these members share values and standards of conduct which have been developed as part of the learner's professional integrity.

A good introduction and brief conceptual analysis showing a logical link between 'profession' and 'develop'.

In contrast to the amateur, the professional practices his or her profession to required standards and for remuneration. It is not possible to attain the required standard without the development of relevant personal and professional skills.

The concept of development implies growth towards the fulfilment of potential. In some contexts this growth to a more advanced state would not require learning or training, but only maturation. An example of this would be the development [growth] of a plant. However, in the context of professional development a more deliberate process of learning is implied. We actively bring about the advance and the fulfilment of potential through successive stages to a higher or more complex level of skill and understanding. Training/Learning is needed for such progress to take place.

A good conceptual point about maturation and intentional development.

From this brief consideration of 'profession and develop' we see that 'professional development' implies more than the acquisition of narrow vocational skills and that the training and learning involves deliberate planning and provision. Moreover, the complex skills required by the professional do not have an end point. They are inherently open to improvement. Thus professional development is on-going. Even while practising a profession, skills can be continuously improved.

Good point.

Thus continuing professional development is important because any learning, including cognitive and personal development, and skill acquisition and improvement, will improve the performance of professional duties.

In short, 'professional development' implies a high level of training, initiation into shared values and standards of conduct, as well as planned and ongoing learning in a variety of learning situations.

Appropriate quote and good reference. Good brief summative conclusion.

Two: Analytic Philosophy

Most social science students are not studying philosophy and will not be doing philosophical essays per se. However, as well as providing some conceptual analysis in your essay, you may also find that you will need to reflect on epistemological questions and think about ethical issues. Epistemology is theory of knowledge. You will sometimes need to reflect on the knowledge status of claims, the accredited sources of knowledge, the validity of reasons and evidence under consideration, etc.

As with other forms of reflection, philosophical analysis is at one remove from experience – a meta-level activity. Interestingly, metaphysics is concerned with the nature of reality and means 'above physics'. Physics studies reality at a concrete, empirical level. Philosophical questions are questions which cannot be answered empirically. In other words, they cannot be answered by the scientific method of observation and experiment. They must be answered through reflection rather than the gathering of data. Philosophical reflection is critical thinking that is, at a very general, abstract level, about these non-empirical questions. There are no right and wrong answers, since such questions are not open to empirical verification or refutation. However, your reflections must not be self-contradictory, and are more plausible if they fit our common human experience and our collective human knowledge. They will gain depth and detail when informed by the work of reputable thinkers.

There are several branches of philosophy. In addition to epistemology and ethics, mentioned above, you may need to give some thought to the philosophical (non-empirical) questions that arise in your particular field of study. For example, psychology students may need to consider the relation between mind and brain, political science students may need to consider the nature of a good society or a good citizen or the meaning of 'democracy' and education students may reflect on the difference between 'education' and 'indoctrination'. Science students may reflect on whether successive generations of scientists are getting nearer to the truth about the world. Theology students might consider what kinds of evidence would justify (at least in part) the claim that God exists. Art students must surely reflect on what we mean by 'art'. Even engineering students might ponder the difference between 'engineering' and 'technology' or 'engineering' and 'science'.

Substantive philosophy uses critical reflection to construct a substantial and thoughtful answer to our questions about leading a good life. Analytic philosophy seeks to analyse non-empirical questions, not so much to construct a substantive answer, but to generate clarity, insight and greater understanding.

To sum up, philosophical reflection is a particular example of critical reflection since it brings critical thinking skills to the task of seeking to answer philosophical (non-empirical) questions.

Ethical Reflection

Ethical reflection is a subset of philosophical questions. Ethical reflection is critical thinking applied to ethical questions and moral dilemmas. Ethics is the branch of philosophy concerned with the nature of moral goodness (meta-ethics) whereas morality is concerned with how we ought to act in particular situations (normative ethics). Associated with moral philosophy is the notion of moral value (moral worth or goodness). Some things are good for their own sake (intrinsic value). Examples include: happiness, knowledge, love, education. Some are good because they are a means of gaining something else (instrumental value). Example: money. Value statements are non-empirical because, unlike factual statements, they do not tell us about the physical world and cannot be tested empirically. Here are some examples of each kind of statement:

Value statements:

- You ought not to steal.
- The use of atomic weapons is wrong.
- Immoral learning is not educational.

Factual statements:

- Metal expands when heated.
- The acute effects of the atomic bombings killed 90,000–146,000 people in Hiroshima.
- I have a headache.

Morality is concerned with how we treat others. It is impossible not to have to make moral judgements and decisions in our day-to-day lives. To behave morally is to count yourself as equal to one person but not more than one. You act as you would wish everyone to act in the same situation. You do not steal, lie or kill and do not wish others to do so. The philosopher Rawls imagined a veil of ignorance before we are born. If you do not know whether you will be disabled or able bodied for example, what sort of society would you hope to find?

I would suggest that the two most significant values of morality are *justice* and *care*. Justice requires that we treat others fairly and equally well, without unfair discrimination. Care requires treating others with empathy and compassion.

Values may be relevant to your essay in a variety of ways. You may, for example, notice that a particular value is implicit in the essay question or that the theory or research data that you are assessing has mistaken a value statement for a factual one. Or you may discern a conflict of our values in a body of work. Educational theory and practice, most of the social sciences, and research projects are all imbued with values, and this will sometimes be reflected as a dimension in your essay work.

Let us consider, then, some examples of epistemological and moral essay reflections:

Moral Considerations

Sample Essay Suggestions: *The national curriculum requires the development of personal, social, moral, educational, cultural and spiritual values. Make some suggestions for a teacher seeking to provide moral education.*

- You will need to begin by setting out what you mean by 'moral education'. Is it defined in the national curriculum? Is this a useful definition? What do you take to be the central aims of moral education? For example: to develop the children's understanding of and commitment to fairness and their empathy/ compassion.
- Perhaps you will say moral education should be part of the curriculum.
- You will need to cover curricula and teaching suggestions. But should moral education have a slot in the timetable or should it permeate the curriculum or both? Discuss moral education in a timetable slot and as permeated throughout the curriculum, and, arguably, in assembly, playtime, clubs, etc. In the timetabled slot you could suggest discussion of moral dilemmas appropriate to the age of the pupils, including perhaps discussion of a dilemma faced by the children themselves.
- You could suggest using stories to provide moral dilemmas and also to develop empathy for the characters.
- You could discuss teaching strategies. For example: discussion may work best with the children seated in a circle. You could touch on the importance of open ended questions and respectfully listening to all points of view.
- You could suggest useful resources. What makes for good resources in this context?
- You might suggest moral education involves personal and social education i.e. the development of some personal characteristics such as fairness, kindness, honesty, etc. and some social virtues such as respect for others, cooperation, etc.
- You could suggest the importance of the teacher setting a good example in their own conduct and creating a classroom ethos conducive to moral behaviour and development. For example: an anti-bullying ethos.
- You could suggest using a variety of pedagogic approaches, to prevent boredom and to cater for the pupils' different learning styles: including experiential games, role-play, brainstorming, group work, individual tasks and using stories with moral role models, etc.
- You must finish with a clear conclusion. Perhaps highlight your key suggestions and link these to your opening conception of moral education.

Epistemological Dimension

> ### Sample Essay: Evaluate the rival claims of X and Y about Z
>
> - To provide a good evaluation you will need to begin with a clear account of the claims of X and Y showing that you understand both sets of claims about Z.
> - You will need to provide a basis for a comparison between X and Y. For example, are you comparing their usefulness for theorists or for practitioners or for researchers? Or are you exploring and comparing the intrinsic strengths and weaknesses – plausibility, elegance, clarity, etc.?
> - In considering their plausibility, you are considering how likely they are to be accurate/valid/true. How justified are the arguments and evidence available and how well supported by your own experience? These are epistemological considerations.
> - On the basis for comparison which you have outlined, you will proceed to compare the rival claims of X and Y in some detail. This is the main body of the essay.
> - In the light of these reflections you can conclude with good reasons for preferring, or rating more highly, either the claims of X or Y about Z.

In seeking to take a critical stance towards your essay question or your proposed answer some searching questions were suggested in Chapter 4. You could now add the following:

- Is the central question a non-empirical one? Are your philosophical reflections convincing, clear, relevant?
- For an empirical question, does the strength of your claims match the strength of your evidence?
- Which values are being assumed in what is claimed? Are these acceptable?
- Is the recommended course of action morally acceptable?
- Does this research generate ethical issues?
- Are there conflicts of value (e.g. honesty vs. kindness)? Can these conflicts be resolved? (You might have to consider possible conflicts of value in an essay on multicultural education, for example.)

Three: Meta-Analysis

Categorisation, Comparisons, Links, Evaluations

When we take an overview of our ground level material, the theories or research data or arguments, we can bring order to it by recognising, or even creating, categories. We break down our material into categories to simplify and organise and thus to better understand it. An example of this categorisation has occurred in our exploration of criticality. We have organised the highly complex, but important, thinking skills which you will find helpful in securing a high grade in your essays, into rational skills, questioning skills and analytic skills.

This presents a very comprehensive toolbox of skills in manageable chunks. These manageable chunks must, however, be sensible groups. In other words, we find subgroups within the material whose members share attributes, and thus form meaningful categories in complex essay material. The members of the rational skills group are all about justification; the members of the questioning skills group (assumptions, context, etc.) are all about probing questions; the members of the analytic group are all meta skills. Similarly, you may be able to recognise or create sensible categories, bringing order and clarity to complexity. This will show that you are in control of your material and understand it.

Comparisons and Links

Within your essay material you may be able to see significant similarities and differences between, or make links between, theories or research projects or the ideas of several recognised thinkers in the field, etc. Such comparisons and links often generate insight, and again you demonstrate control and understanding of the material. For example, we have noticed a similarity between Schön's notion of a reflective practitioner and the idea of reflective critical thinking . This recognition adds to our understanding of Schön and also provides us with an example of critical thinking in action.

Evaluation

Through an evaluation we assess the value or worth of something. For an essay, or part of an essay, you may be asked to evaluate or assess an idea, an argument, a piece of research or a written contribution to our understanding of something. You must consider how you will measure the value of what you are evaluating. For example, think about its purpose and how well it fulfils this. Or perhaps you will measure it by comparing it against a rival or alternative idea, argument or writer's work.

This kind of estimation of worth will involve a critical reflection. Indeed, it is only possible to assess/evaluate your essay material if you have reflected critically on it. You have explored the epistemological base (the evidence and arguments) and employed questioning reflection about assumptions, alternatives, context, etc. You have also used meta-reflection (categorising, contrasting, comparing, making links). Thus, you have asked questions such as:

- Is the ground level material coherent?
- Do I agree/disagree with what is being presented or argued? Why?
- What evidence is cited and is it sound?
- Do other writers and researchers agree?
- How sound are counter arguments or contra indicative research?
- What assumptions are being made?
- What is the context?
- Are there alternative viewpoints and perspectives?
- Were this writer's sources of knowledge recognised and credible sources of knowledge?
- Is the material ethical (e.g. fair, honest, etc.)?
- What are its implicit values?
- How well organised is the material?
- How well does it stand up to comparison with other relevant material?
- Taken overall – how useful is this argument or theory? Why?

Four: Metacognition

Metacognition is second order thinking about our own thinking and learning processes. It is thus both reflexive and reflective. Reflecting on how we learn and how we understand enables us to improve our learning because we can become more aware of and more critical about our own thinking. This awareness will indirectly help you to improve your essay work. In addition, you may be given an essay that directly requires metacognition. For example, you may be asked at the end of a module (or after writing a long essay, or doing a project) to write 500 words (or 1,000 words...) reflecting on your learning. It is important that you keep a sufficient focus on your own learning and that you do not merely write about learning in general. Rather (perhaps after a brief description of the module) provide an overview of your own learning in working through the module. What learning approaches were taken (e.g. group discussions, essay work, etc.) and which were most productive for your understanding and why, and which were less fruitful and why? How could your learning and thinking be improved? If what you are saying links with the literature on learning you can make reference to this relevant reading. You should also order your reflexive material into a coherent and structured piece of work.

Don't be daunted by the need for metacognition. Ideas about your own learning processes will emerge, providing you keep your focus on the meta-cognitive nature of the essay question or task.

Sample Essay: *Metacognitive Reflections*

In approximately 600 words, reflect on your learning during the module on equal opportunities.

Reflecting on my learning during the module on equal opportunities gave me insights into my own preferred learning subjects and learning styles, and I was surprised that these insights had not occurred to me prior to this deliberate reflexive activity. I recognised that I learn best from group discussions. It was information and ideas generated in our group discussions that I retained more vividly than material from books, speakers and videos, interesting though these had been. Similarly, I noticed that it was the abstract material – the theories and ideas, rather than more factual material – which I could most readily recall. I realised that I must make a special effort to memorise such things as dates or figures, though to learn where to find such factual material is also useful!

As I am training to be a teacher I have found that thinking about learning styles has reinforced the importance of using a variety of pedagogic approaches, as was done in the equal opportunity module. This is important because in a class of students there will be a range of preferred learning styles.

It was only in looking back across the module that I explicitly understood the two reasons why it has been an exciting learning journey. Firstly, the module material had generated in me a perspective transformation (Mezirow). I had previously not understood the notion of institutionalised discrimination, as explained in the Swann report, for example. The Swann Report defines institutional racism as the way in which established social practices in social institutions can unwittingly discriminate against minority groups (The Swann Report, 1985). This changed my attitudes from those of an individual who wants to behave well to all individuals, to those of an individual who also understands that discrimination and exclusions against members of minority groups occurs unintentionally, as well as intentionally, through social practices, and not only through individual bad behaviour. Therefore, some of the established routines of schools, the law, health provision, police practices etc. need to change. Similarly, I had not understood the social model of disability. This has changed my attitude to people with disabilities from an attitude of a well-meaning, possibly patronising, individual to the attitude of someone who recognises

A good opening which does indeed show your insights into your own preferred learning subjects and styles.

You draw a constructive implication for your subsequent professional practice.

You link well in this paragraph to the literature whilst remaining focused on your essay question (Mezirow; Swann; Abberley).

disability rights and the oppression of people with disabilities. (Abberley, 1987) The use of the word *apartheid* to describe bussing children away from neighbourhood schools to special schools now seems appropriate, rather than shocking, which was the initial impact on me when it was used by a visiting speaker!

Secondly, learning about the hurtful and disadvantaging effects prejudice and discrimination had on the lives of minority groups and women had, I realised on reflection, brought with it a commitment to be vigilant in recognising my own prejudices and a commitment to guard against unwitting discrimination in my own personal relationships. Moreover, once qualified, I will bring these commitments to my career as a teacher. These commitments, I believe, will ensure that I go on learning more about equal opportunities and inclusive education and that this will be a continuing professional development which will help me to be a better teacher (Day, 1999).

Your ongoing commitment to learning in this area is commendable. Do not neglect learning to recognise structural discrimination.

I have also seen, through my reflections, that this module and the learning it has generated has been deeply significant for my own personal and professional development. Moreover, in undertaking this short piece of work I have recognised that reflecting on my own learning has generated useful further learning and Insights and that, therefore, metacognition is a practice which I should continue to employ and develop.

An appropriate conclusion with a sound point made about metacognition.

Negative and Positive Approaches

A lack of analysis in your essay will not help you to show the criticality which is valued in HE. Essays containing rational argument, critical questioning and use of one of the various forms of analysis will achieve high grades. Without these aspects essays will be largely descriptive and will fail to demonstrate such good characteristics as conceptual clarity and insightful evaluation. They will earn comments such as:

Sample Negative Comments

- Your essay is largely descriptive. You could have compared and evaluated the two positions that you describe.
- You have failed to evaluate the research project, yet part two of the essay question asks for your assessment of it.

- You make some good points about learning but wander from the focus on your own learning which the essay question is about.
- Your essay is confused in parts, mainly because you have not analysed your key terms.

In this chapter you have learned how to be analytic. Analytic skills are important in Higher Education. Including some analysis in your essay will help you to achieve a high grade and your essay will gain comments such as:

Sample Positive Comments

- Your opening analysis of lifelong learning is clear and fits well with the argument in the body of the essay.
- The categories that you use to organise the different styles of leadership in this context bring out their key strengths and weaknesses. This gives you a basis for a rational comparative assessment of their merits. Well done.
- A well-written and well-organised essay with some original ideas.
- Your insightful and interesting exploration of your own learning journey add depth to the essay and demonstrate that you are indeed a reflective practitioner. You have gained a useful understanding of your own learning style.

Brief Exercises

Practise Making Conceptual Distinctions

Write a short piece distinguishing between 'education' and 'indoctrination'.
Write a short piece distinguishing between 'science' and 'engineering'.

Meaning

Ask yourself:

What do we mean by 'category'?

What do we mean by 'metacognition'?

Feedback can be found in Appendix 4.

Conclusion

We have explored four forms of analysis. You will not use every one of these in each of your essays. As we have seen, some essays will require more analysis of its central or tricky abstract concepts than others. Metacognition is most relevant to the essays involving personal learning reflections. However, together with the rational reflections of Chapter 3 and the questioning reflections of Chapter 4, every essay you write should draw on some of these higher order skills. In other words, to count as being more than merely descriptive, your essay will draw on at least one form of justification for its claims *or* use at least one of the aspects of critical thinking *or* engage in one form of analysis. Indeed, if you draw on each category of criticality (rationality, critical questioning, analysis) so much the better!

Summary of Key Points

Do not be worried by the idea of analysis. It simply requires you to take an overview of your material to see it in a new, more holistic way.

The following four kinds of analysis can each be useful for your essays.

1. Conceptual analysis

    - Use quotation marks to indicate that you are talking about a concept and not a thing. You use these when you have not indicated that you were talking about the concept by using the term concept.

      E.g. 'Education' means *worthwhile learning*.
      The concept of education implies that the learning taking place is worthwhile.

    - Abstract concepts are abstract ideas – mental categories such as truth, beauty, education, morality, health, business, engineering and criminality.
    - It is abstract concepts which we analyse in essays to get clear about what they mean.
    - Think about how we use the abstract term in a variety of contexts – this is an overview, a meta-level look at its uses, what it includes and excludes.
    - What key distinctions does the abstract concept make?
    - Many essays benefit from clarification of their key terms. They may require a brief definition. Some essays will require more than this. The abstract term may have a variety of meanings/uses and you will distinguish between these and say which one is relevant to your essay and why.
    - We provide an example of a brief analysis of 'professional development' on page 80.

2. Meta-analysis

    - You take an overview of material in order to organise it, to see new connections, to recognise its strengths and weaknesses or to compare and contrast it with other material. (Advice on how to do these things is given on pages 85 to 87.)
    - Think of analysis as looking down on your material to see it as a whole and therefore to notice more details. This is like seeing more about a terrain when you have a map which takes an overview of it.

(Continued)

(Continued)

3. Philosophical analysis

- Philosophical questions cannot be answered scientifically i.e. through experience, observation, experiment. They require reflection.
- For some essays even non-philosophy students may need to reflect on non-scientific questions that arise in their field. For example psychology students may need to consider the relationship between brain and mind while students of political science may need to think about the nature of the good society or the meaning of democracy.
- Most essays are concerned with some form of knowledge. You are trying to write a true/valid essay. You may need to reflect on how valid your reasons and evidence are. (The branch of philosophy concerned with knowledge is called epistemology.)
- Your essay may require some ethical reflection.
- Ethical reflection is critical thinking applied to ethical questions and moral dilemmas. Your essay may involve a moral dilemma, or a discussion about right and wrong, or about treating people with fairness (justice) and compassion.
- Values may be relevant to your essay in various ways. A particular value may be implicit in the essay question. Or some research may present a value statement as a statement of fact.
- Moral and epistemological sample essays are outlined on pages 84 and 85.

4. Metacognition

- Metacognition is analysis of your own learning and thinking.
- Being critically reflective about our own learning may help us to improve it.
- Some essays require metacognition, e.g. *Write 500 words reflecting on your learning from doing your last essay.* Or: *Write 5,000 words on your learning during this module.*
- There is a sample of a short metacognitive essay on page 88.

For chapter exercise feedback, further reading ideas and more tips on polishing your assignment, check out the appendices at the back of the book.

References

Abberley, P. (1987) *Disability and Oppression*. Warwick: University of Warwick, Department of Sociology.

Day, C. (1999) *Developing Teachers: The Challenges of Lifelong Learning*. London: Routledge/Falmer.

The Swann Report (1985) *Education for All. The Report of the Committee of Enquiry into the Education of Children from Ethnic Minority Groups*. London: HMSO.

The Chambers Dictionary (1998) Edinburgh: Chambers Harrap Publishers Ltd.

Wittgenstein L. (1922) *Tractatus Logico-Philosophicus*. New York: Harcourt, Brace & Co.

Wittgenstein, L. (1953) *Philosophical Investigations*. Oxford: Blackwell Publishing.

6
Originality

Introduction

Imagine that you are the assessor. You face a large pile of essays to be marked. They all say much the same things, drawing on the same material and putting forward the same arguments. Assessment becomes a repetitive and a rather boring task. It certainly adds interest when you come across an essay which has a fresh perspective or some new ideas or arguments or, simply, some striking examples or insights. A touch of originality is likely to gain you some marks. This does not mean that you must have the originality of one of the great thinkers such as Einstein, Newton or Kant. To be original in your essay simply requires a fresh element, however small. In this chapter we will explore these elements. In other words, we will show you several ways in which you could bring a touch of originality to your work. You do not need to use every one of these ways in each essay. Sometimes you will have been original without thinking about this by drawing on a paper or a research project when no-one else in your cohort has discovered it, or its relevance has not been recognised.

Form Your Own Point of View

We have already seen that forming your own point of view goes hand in hand with critical thinking. Having a new point of view makes for a very original essay. However, you must present a plausible viewpoint and justify it with reasons, argument or evidence. It is also perfectly acceptable to agree with the point of view of the essay question, or one of the main thinkers, provided that you acknowledge this and give a reason for accepting it. This reason is your own and in itself brings an element of originality to the essay, as well as demonstrating that you have a point of view and that it is a reasonable and justified one. It may be that you can amend the established viewpoint, in a small way, or that you can add to it. Such modifications or additions also bring in an original element. For example, in the sample essay on critical thinking in Chapter 4, the writer developed a conception of critical thinking such that part of this was identical to the conception of the main thinker, Brookfield, but which had some well-supported additions. Thus, the student properly answered the essay question, and also, at the same time developed their own original point of view.

Use Your Professional Experience

If you are a mature student, you may well have relevant work experience to draw on. Use this. It is an advantage not shared by the younger students. For example, a mature student on a Certificate of Education course may have been a classroom support worker. They will have considerable relevant experience of, for instance, hearing the children read.

Drawing on existing professional experience is particularly useful for students who are on a course for professional development, where previous experience will similarly be directly relevant. Thus, a nurse on a professional development module drew on her own recent experience as a patient. Her essay was about combining a caring approach with professional detachment and she highlighted several small gestures on the part of her nurses that made her feel listened to and less alone, and, simultaneously, she felt herself to be in capable hands.

Use Your Voluntary Work

The student coming to university straight from school or college, and certainly after a gap year, may have relevant experience from their voluntary work or interesting hobbies. You can draw on this for reasons, arguments and examples. For example, your voluntary work at a youth centre may be relevant to an essay about youth work. Or your experiences in Africa, during your gap year, may be relevant to an essay about developing countries.

Many students have experience of voluntary work, which is becoming an advantage when they apply for a place at university. This experience can often be used to enhance an essay. For example, a student helping out at a self-help group for families with children who had Tourette Syndrome used her experiences with the group in an essay on voluntary work. Another student used his experience of visiting speakers to a voluntary group in an essay on community education.

Use Your Personal Experience

Your own personal and family experience may be relevant to some essays. For example, you may have a severely disabled sibling and your essay may be on special education, and your family experience may be relevant. One student, in an essay on disability and the family, drew on her own experience of growing up as the sibling of a severely disabled brother. She also drew on the literature to demonstrate that her own experience was shared and recognised. This personal (yet supported) material added interest and an original element. Another student, writing an essay on institutional racism, used her previous work for an anti-racist organisation in Handsworth, Birmingham to telling effect. She anonymised her case study notes to provide real life examples of the negative effects of institutional practices on individuals who had sought assistance from her organisation. These examples were particularly interesting because they were presented as drawn from real life, but since their point was to illustrate and explain institutional racism in practice, their anecdotal nature did not invalidate this original material.

If you draw on your own experience in producing an argument or theory or in developing your own point of view or in the reasons and evidence and examples that you provide, then this material will be fresh and original.

Your experience is not identical to that of your fellow students. By drawing on your experience the material becomes, in this respect, different from the material in the essays in the rest of the pile. However, personal experience will not be appropriate in some essays. For example, it would not be appropriate in an essay requiring you to identify and evaluate the objective evidence on a topic. If you are unsure, discuss this with your tutor.

Although drawing on your own experience can bring a fresh note to your essay, be careful not to overgeneralise. One family's experience does not establish a universal truth. In general, your own experience is not sufficient to fully justify an argument or, on its own, support a claim. However, it can be used to illustrate a point or to provide a telling example.

Similarly, a brief and well-chosen anecdote may make for interesting illustrative material, but anecdotes should not be overused or used to overgeneralise. They are not an accredited source of knowledge. Look at the anecdote used in *The Meaning of Words* below. In fewer than 80 words an anecdote is used which is interesting and directly relevant. It actually illustrates a problem with the theory being rejected by Wittgenstein, and fits the new theory he went on to develop. This anecdote also provides variety and structure in an otherwise highly abstract piece. Thus, there were several reasons to include it. The point is that anecdotes can certainly enliven and individualise your work, but you must ensure that they are concise, relevant, illuminating and intrinsically interesting.

Sample Anecdote

The Meaning of Words

Do you wonder, as a writer, how the words you choose and set on the icy page carry meaning to your reader? The great modern philosopher, Ludwig Wittgenstein, gave two very different accounts of how words are meaningful. In the *Tractatus Logico-Philosophicus* (1922), he set out, in clear and logical detail, what one might call the commonsense explanation, the picture theory of meaning. A word's meaning is the object for which it stands. The word paper stands for this object in my hand, from which I am reading. The sentence, 'the paper is in my hand' is meaningful by picturing a possible fact in the world, the position (in) of the object (paper) and another object (hand).

Some years later Wittgenstein bumped into a colleague and asked about a mutual acquaintance. The man brushed his own chin. That gesture, in that part of that country at that time, meant that their mutual acquaintance was a 'cuckold'. That is to say, the man's wife was, unknown to her husband, being unfaithful to him. 'Oh, Oh!' thought Wittgenstein, 'My theory of language must be wrong. How can a simple gesture picture such a complex set of facts in the world?'

Wittgenstein then developed his very different theory of meaning, worked out and conveyed in his *Philosophical Investigations* (1953). The meaning of a word (or gesture) lies in its use – its role in an established human practice, what Wittgenstein called a 'language-game'.

The *Tractatus* and the *Philosophical Investigations* are as different in style as they are in ideas about language. The *Tractatus* is orderly and logical and spare with the beauty of a skeleton. The *Philosophical Investigations* is vivid, eclectic, full of metaphor and images with the deliberate repetitions of often approaching the same place from a variety of directions. Both books have been enormously influential.

Use Fresh Material

When you and your fellow students are given an essay title, most of you will draw on the same material in constructing your answer. You will have been given the same reading list. You will have attended the same lectures and taken part in the same discussions. It will not be surprising, therefore, if much of the material you produce in your essays is similar. Some students will draw on the literature more fully, will produce a more coherent essay structure and take a more critical stance than will other students. Nevertheless, the material being structured and critiqued is broadly the same material across the cohort of students. Your essay will gain a considerable original edge if, in addition to the standard and probably essential material, you can also include some fresh material of your own.

For example, you may have come across a book, or part of a book, or a paper, or a professional journal, or a newspaper article which, though it is not on your reading list, is both highly relevant to your essay and creditable. If you use this fresh material in conjunction with the material your tutor expects you to show that you know about, then you will have added something original to your essay.

You may also come across relevant additional ideas from a non-literature sources. For example, you may see a link with material from a different module. Or you might watch a relevant and well-produced TV documentary or watch related TED Talks videos which often include presentations by renowned experts across a wide range of subjects.

Presentations that have been recorded or produced digitally using software such as SlideShare and shared on social media platforms like LinkedIn may also provide supplementary sources and information. Experts and academics often use these digital tools. In the business world, for example, leadership and marketing experts such as Seth Godin, Arianna Huffington, Sheryl Sandberg, Anthony Robbins, Marissa Mayer, Belinda Gates and Guy

Kawasaki all use digital tools to share and promote their work. Be mindful of applying the criteria of credibility and reliability, however, when using these additional or complementary sources.

Be alert for such additional inputs and connections.

Use New Perspectives, Insights, Links and Combinations

Occasionally, and especially when you are particularly interested in the essay subject, you may be gifted with a reorientation of thinking which produces a new perspective for your essay. This will make for an original piece of work. Be careful to show that you do know and understand the established perspective. In a more minor key, without needing a complete perspective transformation, you may, nevertheless, have a new insight or make a new link or create a new amalgam.

A particular insight while doing an MA led to Mal's PhD area. This insight was: 'Even God's view of the world is relative to a consciousness, namely God's'. This insight led Mal to consider different forms of relativism and the implications of these for multicultural education. To what extent are forms of thought and value judgements relative to a cultural context and which elements, if any, are valid in any context?

A link with Bourdieu's notion of social capital (Bourdieu, 1986), made by a student doing an essay about a mental health forum, enabled her to reconcile two apparently conflicting aims of the forum: self-help for the individual member on the one hand, and facilitating social change on the other. This added to the criticality of the essay by bringing in and exploring the notion of social capital, and since this was the only essay to make this link, it added some originality:

> Moreover, the notion of social capital can reconcile two underlying aims of the forum which in some contexts are seen as in opposition. The forum network aims to help the individuals who form it, a distinctively person-centred approach. It also aims for social change to improve policy and practice for those with mental health issues. **Individual** mental health needs are addressed through mutual self-help in the forum, but also their **collective** voice is used in pursuit of social improvements in mental health policy and provision.

Sample Essay: *Cultural context influences engineering practice: Discuss*

The following text is part of an essay. The student began with some analysis of 'cultural context' and 'engineering practice'. He went on to identify several ways in which cultural factors had influenced engineering designs. Notice, however, that in the section of the essay quoted, the examples given of differences between US and Western European designs help us to understand the point being made. They also bring some originality to the essay because different engineering students would choose different examples.

Extract

It is often assumed that engineering practice transcends cultural influence; that the best engineering practice will emerge from the interface between the engineering problem and the real world, mediated by mathematical models and physics (the constraints of the real world). However, culture and engineering interact such that engineering, over time and between societies, is influenced by cultural context.

Well expressed. You convey complex ideas very clearly. You introduce the claim that in spite of the constraints of the real world, on engineering tasks, cultural factors influence engineering solutions.

In the USA, the emphasis is often on simplicity, reliability, and cost effectiveness. It was in the USA that the idea of a single water tap in the middle of the sink for both hot and cold water first came into being. In Western Europe the emphasis tends to be on the product being elegant and a pleasure to use. This is very apparent in the recent spate of new designs of elaborate and expensive cork removers for wine bottles that are appearing in our shops.

Useful examples.

Some might say that such differences are the product of fashion. However, unlike dress, furniture or buildings some engineering work is rarely, if ever, seen. Inside the average American car is a large, simple, reliable engine, with bland and boring characteristics. Inside the average European car is a small, highly-tuned responsive engine that delights the driver by its responsiveness. The number of broken down vehicles that often used to be seen on European motorway hard shoulders was a testament to the resulting lack of reliability. Something in the European culture led engineers and users to choose a design that was less reliable than it could be for the pleasure derived from its use. Similarly, cultural factors influence the relative weighting given to considerations of the risk versus the expense of a particular design solution.

To discount the influence of fashion, the choice of hidden car engines contrasting with clothes furniture and buildings is a good choice. It illustrates your point clearly.

(Continued)

(Continued)

Even in an apparently hard-edged practice like engineering we see that there isn't just one solution, but a family of best solutions, and which of these we prefer will be partly conditioned by cultural factors. For instance, an electrical connection from a shore based mains power supply to a ship in a western dockyard is by a very large electric plug and socket. In the Russian dockyards there is no plug and socket and the connection is by individual wires with each one poked into a screw terminal. Either solution is equally efficient.

The case for the influence of cultural factors is well made by citing cultural factors influencing choice from a family of best solutions. This is followed by an effective example. Well done.

Negative and Positive Approaches

You may produce a competent essay and gain a pass mark. To achieve a high grade, however, you need something extra, such as the criticality discussed in the last few chapters or a touch of originality as explored in this one. Without this extra ingredient you could gain comments such as the following:

Sample Negative Comments

- This is a competent, if unexciting essay.
- Some interesting illustrations or examples would have made your points clearer and at the same time would have enlivened the essay.
- You do not say why you agree with Brookfield.
- You could have made good use of the interesting and relevant experience that you described in our group discussions.

In this chapter we have looked at ways in which you can give your essay or assignment an element of originality. This does not mean you need an outlandish viewpoint or a revolutionary new breakthrough idea. An arresting example, an unusual but reasonable argument, or drawing on your own experience will all add an interesting difference and can gain you some extra marks and some positive comments such as:

Sample Positive Comments

- The examples you use are useful and interesting.
- The professional experience you draw on adds much to your essay.

- Your point of view is unusual but well supported. Well done.
- Your original perspective on the controversy is useful, arresting and convincing. A very good piece of work.

Brief Exercises

Practise Some Original (Lateral) Thinking

Think of 10 different ways of using each of the following: a brick; a book; a cup; a pen; a biscuit.

Original Elements

Write down two ways in which your essay can demonstrate originality.

Feedback is given in Appendix 4.

Conclusion

We have looked at some of the ways in which you can 'lift' your essay from the 'pile' by bringing in an original element. Provided this original material is included in addition to, rather than instead of, the material you are expected to discuss, and provided it is relevant, it will usually enhance your essay. However, if you are unsure that the material you want to use is appropriate, you could discuss this with your tutor before using it.

Do not overuse the techniques discussed in this chapter and do not over-generalise or over claim. However, original ideas, fresh points of view and personal examples will often be part of the most interesting work.

Summary of Key Points

1. A touch of originality in your essay adds interest and could therefore gain you additional marks.
2. You do not have to have the originality of Einstein. A fresh element, such as a good example from your own experience, can enliven your essay.
3. Having your own point of view is important in an essay. It may be more or less original but should always be well supported. Or it may be that you can provide a new argument in support of an established point of view. Or your originality could simply be in the form of having modified the existing view in a fresh way.

(Continued)

(Continued)

4. You may have professional, personal or voluntary work experience that is relevant to your essay. Drawing on this will bring new material into your essay.
5. A well-chosen, brief anecdote may provide an interesting illustration. Do not overuse this as evidence in support of a claim but use it to illustrate what you are saying.
6. Most students who have been set the same essay title will be drawing on the same reading list and lectures. Your answers will all be similar and may become a bit boring for the assessor. Fresh relevant material, added to that which you are expected to show that you are familiar with, will add interest/originality.
7. Fresh material could be from a book or article not on your reading list but which is nevertheless relevant and creditable.
8. You may see a relevant link with material from another module which you are taking, or have taken.
9. You may be gifted with a fresh insight or with that reorientation of thinking which will give you a new perspective on your essay.
10. Simply drawing on your own experience is likely to produce different reasons and different examples from those of others in your group, because they have different experiences.
11. Personal experience alone is not evidence for a claim but could be used to illustrate a point. It is not appropriate for all essays. If in doubt, discuss this with your tutor.
12. Any one of these ways of bringing in a new element to your essay will give some originality. You do not need to use all of them in one essay!

For chapter exercise feedback, further reading ideas and more tips on polishing your assignment, check out the appendices at the back of the book.

References

Bourdieu, P. (1986) *The Forms of Capital* in J.C Richardson (ed.) *Handbook of Theory of Research for the Sociology of Education.* Westport, CT: Greenwood.

Wittgenstein, L. (1922) *Tractatus Logico-Philosophicus.* New York: Harcourt, Brace & Company.

Wittgenstein, L. (2001 [1953]) *Philosophical Investigations.* Oxford: Blackwell.

7

Presentation and Academic Conventions

Introduction

In this chapter we consider the professional presentation of your work. Good presentation and good English contribute to a good grade. We also show you how to use the academic conventions, such as acronyms, quotations, references, etc. You are not born knowing the correct use of these, but correct use gives a good impression, and that good impression may well influence your grade.

You can lose or gain marks for the presentation of your work. You may even lose more marks than the substance of your essay warrants because we are all more influenced by appearance then we tend to realise, including assessors. Do not use complicated folders, ribbons or pictures and illustrations on the front cover. A good initial impression is created with a simple, professional and easy-to-read presentation of your essay. Check if there are department guidelines on the presentation of your work and follow these to the letter. If there are no such guidelines, ask your tutor for advice.

Use Good Principles of Presentation and Style

In the absence of guidelines from your tutor, college or university, apply the following presentation principles:

- **Fonts:** Use a 12 point font for the main body of your text and no less than an 11 point font. Choose a font that is popular such as a plain serif (Times New Roman) or a sans serif (Arial). These are widely accepted fonts, although some universities do have their own very specific preferences. (A tutor may allow a dyslexic student to use his or her preferred font.) Do check this. Differentiate your headings in different sized fonts so that your essay is easy to navigate.
- **Line spacing:** Use at least 1.5 line spacing and ideally double line spacing when presenting your essay. This allows the assessor space to mark your essay.
- **Margins:** If there are no specific guidelines on margins, use a minimum of 2.5 cm all round and a maximum of 3 cm all round. Generally, a wider left-hand margin will allow for any binding.
- **Pagination:** Use page numbers, generally in the bottom right hand corner in the footer. Page numbers need to be clear and easy to follow. For larger bodies of work that have an automatically generated contents page, remember to check that your page numbers correspond before final submission.
- **Content formatting:** Check that all the sections of your content flow correctly and that there are no headings left hanging at the bottom of a page. Move these on to the next page to ensure the flow of text. Section breaks can be easily inserted into your document.
- **Binding:** For shorter essays, neatly staple your document before you hand it in. For longer pieces of work, use binding to present your work professionally. Simple spine binders with plastic or cardboard covers give a document a good finish.
- **Quality of paper:** Although it is not essential to use a higher grade of paper than 80gsm, it will give your document a more professional feel if you use a slightly thicker grade (90 or 100gsm). Also, print on white paper. Don't use coloured paper unless this is specific to your work. The aim is to appear highly professional, not attention-seeking.

Presenting your work professionally demonstrates that you have paid attention to the details and that you have taken pride in what you have produced, which will make a difference to your grade as presentation often forms a percentage of the marks given.

Use Correct English

A good piece of work is marred by language errors of spelling, punctuation and grammar. An otherwise good piece of work will lose marks for this, and a poor piece may well slip down into a fail grade. If you need help with your written English, the university may provide classes.

Always proofread your completed essay for grammatical and typographical errors. And, of course, you should make use of the spellcheck facility on your computer. In particular, check that you have written in complete sentences, each with a subject and a verb and an object and a full stop.

An essay is a formal piece of work. Do not use slang or contractions such as 'don't' and do not overuse bullet points which are not a substitute for formal discussion. Do not try to sound intellectual and 'academic'. You will merely sound pompous. Try to write the claims of your essay and each sentence of it as clearly and unambiguously as possible.

A common error is the misused apostrophe. If you are not sure about using apostrophes correctly, master it once and for all in Appendix 2. Correct use of the apostrophe gives a good impression of someone in control of their work. Appendix 2 also gives brief advice about the use of the colon and semicolon. If you are unsure of other aspects of punctuation, or if you are unsure about good grammar, there are books which will teach you. For example you could consult *Academic Writing and Grammar for Students* (Osmond, 2015). (A brief review of this is given in Chapter 8.) Also useful, and written with humour, is Lynn Truss' *Eats, Shoots and Leaves* (2003).

For good communication with your reader, on the whole you should not use overlong sentences or very long paragraphs. A paragraph contains the development of one particular thought. A long paragraph may well have developed two ideas and a very short paragraph may well have failed to fully develop any point at all.

If you have exceeded the word length required for your essay, check it for any repetition you may have unwittingly included. In addition, do a pruning job. Most work is actually improved when we cut out unnecessary words; 'unnecessary words' do not add anything to the meaning of the sentence. You may be surprised to find how many words you save by cutting out such 'wasted' words.

For example:

> A good essay will not contain far too many language mistakes and errors which will give a bad impression to the tutor who is marking it. (26 words)

> A good essay will not contain so many language errors that it gives a poor impression to the assessor. (19 words and a better sentence)

If you have not produced sufficient words, do not try to pad out your essay with irrelevant material or 'wasted' words. Instead, think hard about each part of your answer. What aspects would benefit from further work? What ideas would benefit from clarification? What other thinkers have had different or additional points to make?

Make sure that you have included the essay title at the top of your essay. Do not change this in any way. For example, do not shorten it, or put it in your own words. Having the accurate title there will help to keep you focused on it, and if your group has had several choices of essay question it may also be helpful to the assessor.

Finally, if your department requires a submission sheet with your essay, make sure that you have included it and that you have entered all the details required.

Use Academic Conventions Correctly

It is important to use the correct academic conventions. Do so from the start and they will soon become second nature and help your work to give a good impression to the academic reader. And it is not only about a good impression. If you are found to have plagiarised, for example, your essay may well be disqualified. If you reference incorrectly, you may well lose considerable marks. In what follows we will cover: plagiarism, acronyms, the use of tables and diagrams, the use of quotations and quotation marks and, last but by no means least, correct referencing.

Avoid Plagiarism

Plagiarism is using someone else's work without acknowledging this. You are passing off another's work as your own (Neville, 2010). This may be done deliberately, as with copying some text without reference, or even by buying a ready-made essay. However, it can also occur unwittingly. After you have read something, perhaps several times, and assimilated this so that it becomes part of your own thinking, you may reproduce it, unthinkingly, as part of the flow of your own ideas.

Plagiarism is often noticed by the assessor. The plagiarised section may be markedly different in style from the student's or the assessor may simply recognise this particular piece. Some universities use software to detect plagiarism. Minor plagiarism may result in your having to resubmit your essay with a cap on the mark awarded. Serious plagiarism may even lead to a student having to leave their course.

You are reading this book because you want to produce a good essay and you are not likely to plagiarise on purpose. We will focus, therefore, on how to avoid accidental plagiarism.

a. When you want to use the work of another be sure to reference this correctly. If you want to make use of lengthy material, do not quote long sections, but do not copy it all down unacknowledged. Simply explain in your own words what the writer has said, perhaps with a significant short quotation from their work, and acknowledging the source of the material/ideas.
b. In Chapter 1, you were advised to make notes of your reading in preparation for your essay. This should enable you to know who has said what and enable you to reference accurately.
c. If you have written something in your essay which you feel you have read, but which you cannot place you can say...... *Some writers have argued that......* and then rewrite the section without looking at it so that the actual expression of the ideas is your own.
d. If you are still unsure that you have not avoided plagiarism, you could use a software package on your own work.

Use Acronyms Correctly

An acronym is a group of capital letters which are accepted as standing for a group of words.

For example, BBC is an accepted abbreviation (acronym) for the British Broadcasting Corporation. HE is recognised as an acronym for Higher Education.

The rule for using acronyms in an academic piece of work, such as an essay, is as follows:

The first time you use the group of words for which there is a recognised acronym, place the acronym in brackets immediately after the words. Subsequently, use the acronym without the words. The reader now knows what the acronym stands for.

For example:

• Students in higher education [HE] will be expected to write essays. They may be given three or four essays each year. They will be expected to write these to a standard required in HE.
• The Workers' Educational Association [WEA] offers short courses to working and retired adults. These students gain social as well as educational benefits from attending WEA courses.

Use Tables and Charts Correctly

The rules for the use of tables and charts and other diagrams are also quite simple. Only use a visual representation if the information it provides will aid understanding, or if it can provide the information more concisely than can prose. Introduce the table and give it a number and name.

The following Table 7.1: *Census of the number of hunters in Europe* conveys in just one page, a huge amount of information.

TABLE 7.1   Census of the number of hunters in Europe

	Countries	Km² × 10³	Hunter Numbers	Population × 10⁶	% of Hunters	Pop / km²	Ratio To Pop
	France	643	1,313,000	63.7	2.1	99	1:47
	Germany	357	340,000	82.4	0.4	230	1:241
	Italy	301	750,000	58.1	1.2	193	1:77
	Spain	505	980,000	40.4	2.3	80	1:44
	United Kingdom	245	800,000	60.8	1.3	248	1:74
Nordic Region	Denmark	43	165,000	5.5	3.1	128	1:327
	Finland	338	290,000	5.2	5.8	15	1:17
	Norway	324	190,000	4.6	4.75	14	1:21
	Sweden	450	290,000	9	3.22	20	1:31
Baltic Region	Estonia	45	15,000	1.3	0.1	29	1:100
	Latvia	65	25,000	2.3	1.2	35	1:80
	Lithuania	65	32,000	3.6	0.9	55	1:113
	Poland	313	106,000	38.5	0.3	123	1:363
Atlantic Region	Belgium	31	20,000	10	0.2	323	1:500
	Ireland	70	350,000	4.1	8.9	59	1:12
	Luxembourg	3	2,000	0.4	0.5	133	1:200
	Netherlands	42	26,500	16.6	0.1	395	1:626
Central European Region	Austria	84	115,000	8.2	1.4	98	1:70
	Czech Republic	79	110,000	10.2	1.1	129	1:91
	Hungary	93	54,500	10	0.5	108	1:183
	Slovakia	49	55,000	5.4	1.1	110	1:100
	Slovenia	20	22,000	2	1	100	1:91
	Switzerland	41	30,000	7.6	0.43	185	1:233

	Countries	Km² × 10³	Hunter Numbers	Population × 10⁶	% of Hunters	Pop / km²	Ratio To Pop
Mediterranean Region	Cyprus	9	45,000	0.8	6.4	89	1:15
	Greece	132	270,000	10.7	2.7	81	1:37
	Malta	0.3	15,000	0.4	3.7	1333	1:27
	Portugal	92	230,000	10.6	2.3	115	1:43
South East Region	Albania	29	17,000	3.6	0.6	124	1:176
	Bosnia Herzegovina	51	50,000	4.6	1.2	90	1:80
	Bulgaria	111	110,000	7.3	1.4	66	1:66
	Croatia	57	55,000	4.5	1.37	79	1:73
	Moldova	34	–	4.3	–	126	–
	Montenegro	14	–	0.7	–	50	–
	Romania	238	60,000	22.3	0.27	94	1:372
	Serbia	88	80,000	10.1	0.7	115	1:137
	Turkey	781	300,000	71.2	0.42	91	1:237

(*Source*: FACE/CIA World Factbook, http://www.face.eu/about-us/members/across-europe/census-of-the-number-of-hunters-in-europe-september-2010.)

Ensure that you provide useful, relevant explanation and discussion of any visual representations which you include. If you have taken these representations from elsewhere, be careful to give the source.

Use Quotations and Quotation Marks Correctly

Quotations

Do not use too many quotations. This gives the impression that you lack confidence in your own ideas. Do not use very long quotations. Where you want to use the work of another, you should explain what they have said in your own words. Reserve quotations for words that are so well expressed, or so memorable or so well known and much quoted that they are worthy of repetition. Where you use your own words, you must still give the reference, which shows that you are using the literature and protects you from the charge of plagiarism. When you do use a quotation, this should be discussed, or at least commented upon, to show that you understand it. When you give the reference for a quotation, you should also give the page number.

For short quotations, enclose the author's words in quotation marks. For longer quotations (three lines or more), introduce it with a colon and set it off

109

in a block quote (indented on both sides). In his useful book about academic writing and grammar, Osmond makes the following point:

> Usually, it is it better to paraphrase than quote directly, because it proves to the reader that you have understood an idea so well that you can express it in your own words. Sometimes, however, a well-chosen quote can illustrate your skill in knowing when someone else has written it best. It is better to have more indirect citation than direct. I tend to recommend that about two thirds of your citations are indirect, and one third direct. (Osmond, 2015: 119)

Use of Quotation Marks

You may want to quote a brief phrase and you can do this simply within your own text provided that you use quotation marks and give the reference. For example:

> Since the work of R.S. Peters we have surely accepted that education is a 'normative' concept, because 'worthwhile' learning is involved (Peters, 1966).

We saw in Chapter 5 that you should indicate with quotation marks when a word refers to a concept and this has not been indicated in the text:

Education is a normative concept.
Peters' understanding of 'education' has been influential.

Use Citations and References Correctly

Where your essay or assignment requires you to refer to the work of others, you will need to use citations and references. A citation is where you refer to someone else's work in the body of your text.
For example:

> It is estimated that wolves first came into contact with humans some 10,000 years ago. We cannot be certain about this, but one of the oldest archaeological sites that contains both human and wolf remains is the Sandia Cave in Las Huertas Canyon, New Mexico (Busch, 1995).

> Midgeley (2003) argues that in order to justify our destructive behaviour towards animals we construct narratives that see them as 'other', as different from ourselves, and often as something that is of lesser value or worth.

In a citation, you will use the name of the author(s) followed by the year of publication, and in some citation styles, the page number where the information you have sourced can be found. The citation is then followed by the bibliographical reference which is usually at the end of the article or book.

There are many different styles for referencing the work of others. Before you choose a style that you prefer, make sure you check the style guide or recommendations from your college or university. Some institutions are quite strict on referencing styles.

However, if there is no specific requirement from your college or university, then you can choose to use one of the more popular styles for citations and referencing. Some of these styles are adopted for specific areas of study. For example, Harvard is often used in humanities subjects, the Vancouver system is used in medical and scientific papers and APA (the American Psychological Association style) is mainly used in the social sciences. Each referencing style will give you examples of how to produce your citations and bibliography references for the different sources of work including books, academic journals, digital sources, reports, articles in edited collections and websites. They will also give guidance on secondary referencing where you may be referring to a source within a source.

Software Tools for Managing Citations and References

It can be a chore trying to keep track of your citations and references. You can, of course, use a manual system such as an index card referencing system. However, technology now provides us with a wide range of free or cost-effective software tools that make the job easier and potentially more accurate too. Most of these also integrate with browsers (e.g. Google Chrome) and word processing software such as Microsoft Word and automatically update your citations and references as you produce your essays and assignments. These are useful tools for longer assignments, but if you adopt them early in your academic studies, you will become familiar with these tools, which will make life easier when you do move on to larger academic projects such as dissertations and theses.

Your university or college library will have information on citation management tools, and an Internet search will also provide you with lists of some of the best programmes and apps that can either be loaded onto your computer or mobile device or accessed via the web. Many of the programs are free for a certain level of use or on a trial basis. Some will require a pro account if you want to use them more extensively.

A few of the more popular tools and programs can be found in the list below, but do your homework and evaluate them to see which ones will suit your needs:

- BibMe – www.bibme.org
- RefDot – this is a Google Chrome extension – simply search RefDot
- Zotero – www.zotero.org
- Mendeley – www.mendeley.com

Be Conscientious About Proofreading

Proofreading your work is very important. It is, however, more difficult to do effectively than you may imagine. It is easy to get sucked into the meaning of the piece and miss typographical and other small errors. Alternatively, one can be so focused on these, that a contradiction or a repetition could be overlooked. You need to macro read for the meaning/content and read again, a micro read, for the typographical errors, grammar and punctuation. Moreover, you may be so familiar with your own thinking for the essay that you read what you think is there rather than what is actually on the page. You have become too close to the material.

Here are some tips for effective proofreading:

- Work through the checklists at Appendix 1.
- This will include:

    o Asking a critical friend (see page 63) or, simply, a literate friend to proofread your essay.
    o Doing a macro read.
    o Doing a micro read.

- Finally, submit your essay on time! This might require you to print your essay and hand it in with a submission sheet, or you may need to submit it online using eSubmissions. (Check with your tutor or university the correct submission format.)

The following short piece, about epistemology and your essay, demonstrates well-presented work, using the academic conventions correctly.

Sample Essay: *Epistemology and your essay*

Epistemology

Epistemology is the branch of philosophy that is concerned with the nature of knowledge. Some understanding of the nature of knowledge is relevant to the academic essay writer because of the assumption that an essay in Higher Education (HE) is seeking to convey (and demonstrate) knowledge about, and understanding of, the subject under discussion.

What, then, is meant by 'knowledge'?

Knowledge

Knowledge is more than mere belief. We may hold a false belief, but, if we claim that we know something then we are claiming that it is true. Even truth is insufficient for knowledge. We might arrive at a true belief by pure guesswork. However, to have knowledge means that we hold a justified true belief.

At HE level it is expected that the claims made by the essay writer will be justified in the essay. In this way the essay is seen to be seeking knowledge and will be assessed as appropriately rational. Indeed, to be rational, the strength of the claims made must fit the strength of the justificatory evidence. For example:

There is little evidence, but it is at least plausible that…

On balance, from the evidence currently available, it seems unlikely that...

The evidence is now substantial. It is no longer irrational to accept this alternative view.

The question that arises, however, is what counts as good evidence. What are the accredited sources of knowledge from which we can derive justified true belief?

The Sources of Knowledge

Primary Sources of Knowledge

Sense Experience

It is through our senses that we learn about the physical world. This is the only avenue by which information about the external world can reach us. We have direct privileged access to our own inner world of sensations such as pain. The more shared and shareable that sense experience is, the more this agreement in experience confers reliability upon it. (An hallucination, for example, is not readily shared and shareable.) This is called empirical evidence; the scientific method of observation and experiment based on sensory experience.

Reason (Logic and Evidence)

Logically true statements provide knowledge. Tautologies and valid deductive arguments based on true premises produce logically true statements.

Secondary Sources of Knowledge

Secondary sources of knowledge are useful and can be drawn upon in an essay. However, this must be done with an awareness that they are secondary sources, which means that they have relied on primary sources. They should be used with caution and lead to qualified, rather than absolute, claims to knowledge.

Authority

We often accept something is true because an authority tells us so. The reliable authority uses primary sources of knowledge. An authority is a useful source for the essay writer,

(Continued)

113

(Continued)

because an easy writer is unable to check everything for themselves. However, the writer should notice the background of the authority and assess the evidence they cite and the arguments they deploy. How credible is this person and are there opposing points of view to consider?

Intuition

Sometimes we have unconsciously noticed things. Or we may have read something in more than one reliable context but do not remember this consciously. Thus, we may have correct intuitions. But we may also have false ones. An intuition must be justified by a primary source of knowledge to count as knowledge.

Forms of Knowledge

Hirst introduced the idea of different forms of knowledge (2010). He introduced seven such forms: 'mathematics, physical sciences, human sciences, history, religion, literature and the fine arts, philosophy' (2010: 35). Hirst argued that each of these distinct forms has four distinguishing features: its own key concepts, for example number and matrix in mathematics and good and ought in morality; its own logical structure, or, in other words, the conceptual structure through which its own aspects of experience are made meaningful to us; distinctive truth criteria through which its claims can be tested against experience, and, finally, its own methods for exploring a particular area of human experience. (2010: 33–34)

Hirst's influential ideas have been critiqued both positively and negatively. For the essay writer, the important point to assimilate is that justified claims do not only rely on sense experience/observation and experiment but also on a variety of forms of valid reasoning and reflection. Mathematics has its own laws. The social sciences are less hard-edged than the physical sciences since, for example, they must recognise that individuals have privileged access to their own inner experiences. History relies on the interpretation of documentary evidence. Religion acknowledges religious experience, revelation and the interpretation of the scriptures. Literature encourages aesthetic appreciation of literary forms and techniques of literary criticism. In other words, there are a variety of VALID ways in which we make sense of our shared experience of our shared physical, social and interpersonal worlds.

What, then, are the implications of these epistemological considerations for the production of good HE level essays? Since such work seeks for knowledge and understanding relevant to the essay question, a concern for rational justification is required. The forms of rational justification will be appropriate to the forms of knowledge implicit in the question. The strength of the claims made should be proportionate to the level of justification offered.

Finally, a good essay usually draws on the appropriate literature. However, students should not accept this literature uncritically. Authority is only a secondary source of knowledge. Writers drawn upon from the literature, to use in an essay, must be thought about critically and used with a rational evaluation.

Negative and Positive Approaches

In this chapter we have shown you how to present your work, emphasised the importance of good English and demonstrated the correct use of acronyms, tables and charts, quotations and quotation marks. We have also given you skills to avoid plagiarism and to be an effective proofreader.

If you do not follow this advice you will receive negative comments on your essays and assignments, such as:

Sample Negative Comments

- I could not read your handwriting. Please type and resubmit.
- The fancy font you use adds nothing and it is it difficult to read. Use Times New Roman or Arial next time.
- Your work is marred by many small errors (spelling mistakes, poor grammar, punctuation errors and typos). This is careless and has cost you marks.
- Learn to reference properly. Your work is let down by omitted citations, inaccurate dates and titles of the books you have cited and inconsistent punctuation of the references.

If you follow the advice in this chapter on presenting your work, your use of English, use of the academic conventions and competent proofreading, you will have the basic requirements for good work. The feedback from your tutor may include positive feedback such as the following:

Sample Positive Comments

- Your work is well presented and well written which adds to the all-round competence of your essay.
- A professional piece of work. Well done.
- Your work has attained a high academic level. As well as presenting a well-organised and well-supported, original point of view, you write well, with full attention to all the academic conventions and with appropriate and well-placed references.
- You provide an excellent reference list. This comes out of the wide and relevant reading which you have clearly demonstrated in this essay.

Brief Exercise: Practise Cutting Wasted Words

Here is an example of a piece reduced from 75 to 50 words.

(a) Social workers work with individuals who are vulnerable and families who are vulnerable to help to improve outcomes in their lives. Social workers often work in teams from several health areas with other health and educational professionals and social workers have a range of tasks such as: protecting people from harm and abuse, supporting people to live independently, being an advocate for people, and giving them information about services they may require and find helpful.

(b) Social workers work with vulnerable individuals and families to help improve outcomes in their lives. They often work in multidisciplinary teams with other health and educational professionals. Their range of tasks include: supporting independent living, being an advocate, protecting people from harm and giving information about services they may require.

Now practise cutting wasted words out of the following short piece. You should manage to reduce this by at least 20 words:

Social workers go into social work because they really want to make a difference to people's lives. They have a desire to work with people and to help them to make their lives better. To be a social worker a person needs an undergraduate degree in social work or a Master's degree in social work and obviously they must also be properly registered with one of the four recognised UK regulators. They need a wide and extensive range of skills and abilities.

An example of this paragraph, reduced by 36 words, is given in Appendix 4.

Conclusion

The contents of this chapter include advice on the presentation of your essay, your standard of written English and your use of the academic conventions. These three elements of your essay are separable from the essay content and apply to every essay you write. They can make a significant difference to the grade your essay achieves. Getting these three aspects right may lift your mark into the next grade; conversely, poor presentation, poor English or incorrect use of academic conventions may result in your essay losing marks and consequently it may drop down a grade. To achieve a high grade in HE, an essay will usually be well presented, well written and with correct use of acronyms, quotations, tables and charts, and referencing.

Summary of Key Points

Good presentation, good English and correct use of the academic conventions contribute to a your essay receiving a good grade.

1. Good presentation

    *   Present your work in a professional way – you don't need to use fancy folders. Follow departmental guidelines on your presentation, to the letter, if they exist. If not, use a 12 point and plain serif font such as Times New Roman or a sans serif font such as Arial.
    *   Differentiate headings in different sized fonts to show the structure of your essay and to allow for easier navigation.
    *   Use at least 1.5 line spacing or ideally double line spacing.
    *   Use a margin of a minimum of 2.5 cm/maximum 3 cm all round.
    *   Use page numbers.

2. Good English

    *   A good piece of work is marred by language errors of spelling, punctuation and grammar.
    *   Take advantage of university classes in written English if you need help and if these are offered.
    *   Do not use slang or contractions such as 'don't'.
    *   Do not overuse bullet points.
    *   Do not try to sound academic. You will merely sound pompous.
    *   Write as clearly and unambiguously as possible.
    *   The correct use of the apostrophe, which is often used wrongly, and the colon and semicolon are described in Appendix 2.
    *   Do not use overlong sentences or very long paragraphs.
    *   If your essay is too long cut any repetitions and any unnecessary words.
    *   If your essay is too short consider which parts would gain by added discussion or added material.

3. Write to the exact title.
4. Complete the submission sheet if this is required.
5. Plagiarism

    *   Do not copy another writer. Explain what they have said in your own words and remember to cite the original.
    *   If you cannot remember who wrote something, say 'some writers have argued that…' and use your own words to reproduce this.

(Continued)

(Continued)

6. Acronyms

  - The first time you use a group of words for which there is a recognised acronym, place the acronym in brackets immediately after the words e.g. Workers' Education Association (WEA). **Subsequently use the acronym alone.**

7. Tables and charts

  - Only use a visual representation if the information it provides will aid understanding, or if it can provide the information more concisely than prose could.
  - Introduce the table and give it a number and a name e.g. Table 7.1: *Census of the number of hunters in Europe.*
  - Place table captions above the table, figure captions below the figure. Do not forget to provide a source for your images or data.

8. Quotations

  - Do not use too many quotations. This gives the impression that you lack confidence in your own ideas.
  - Do not use very long quotations. Where you want to use the work of another, you should explain what they have said in your own words. Reserve quotations for words that are so well expressed, or so memorable or so well known and much quoted that they are worthy of repetition.
  - When you do use a quotation, this should be discussed, or at least commented upon, to show that you understand it.
  - Place short quotations in quotation marks within the text. Introduce longer quotations with a colon, and place, indented, on the next line.

9. Citations and references

  - A citation is where you refer to someone else's work in the body of your text, e.g.: Midgeley (2003) argues that in order to justify our destructive behaviour towards animals we construct narratives that see them as 'other', as different from ourselves, and often as something that is of lesser value or worth.
  - If your department has guidelines about the reference style follow these.
  - If your department does not have a recommended style then use a popular one (e.g. Harvard).
  - Each reference style will give you examples of how to reference books, academic journals, digital sources, reports, articles in edited collections, websites and on referencing a source within a source.
  - If you wish to use these, there are software tools to help keep track of your citations and references (see page 111.)

10. Proofreading

- Proofreading is important and surprisingly difficult.
- First, macro proofread your essay for clarity of meaning, repetition and structure.
- Second, micro proofread for typographical errors, grammar and punctuation.
- Do a spell check.
- You could ask a critical friend to read through your essay, before submitting it, with any required submission sheet, on time.
- Finally, to cover all these checks, you could use the checklists at Appendix 1.

For chapter exercise feedback, further reading ideas and more tips on polishing your assignment, check out the appendices at the back of the book.

References

Busch, R.H. (1995) *The Wolf Almanac: A Celebration of Wolves and Their World*. New York: The Lyons Press.

Hirst, P. (2010) *Knowledge and the Curriculum*. London: Routledge.

Midgely, M. (1984) *Animals and Why They Matter*. Athens, GA: University of Georgia Press.

Neville, C. (2010) *The Complete Guide to Referencing and Avoiding Plagiarism*. Maidenhead: Open University Press.

Osmond, A. (2015) *Academic Writing and Grammar for Students*. London: Sage.

Peter, R.S. (1966) *Ethics and Education*. London: Allen & Unwin.

Truss, L. (2003) *Eats, Shoots and Leaves*. London: Fourth Estate.

8

Other Forms of Assignment

Overview

- Introduction
- Group Work
- Reviews
- Sample Reviews
- Writing Reports
- Research Projects
- Other Forms of Writing
- Negative and Positive Approaches
- Conclusion
- Summary of Key Points
- References

Introduction

Some courses will include other kinds of assignment in addition to essays. These non-essay assignments take many forms. In almost all cases the advice of the first seven chapters of this book will be relevant. You will need to read the literature, plan, organise your work, be rational, critical and analytic, and present well-written work in a professional manner and with the correct referencing and so on. In addition to these characteristics of good HE level work, however, these other forms of assignment have additional requirements of their own. It is these additional requirements which we will consider in this chapter. Because you may not be familiar with these forms of assignment, it will be particularly important that you check the marking criteria for the assignment. What is expected of you? You should also discuss this with your tutor.

Many modules require formative pieces of work to be completed. Formative work is not usually evaluated, although some institutions give a hypothetical grade to enable the student to see how they are doing. Nevertheless, you should use the opportunity to complete formative tasks as they are designed to facilitate learning which will be helpful to you in your graded assignments.

Group Work

Most graded assignments in HE are individual pieces of work completed by an individual student who is given an individual grade. However, in areas of study where team work is important, group work projects may be assessed. Assessments may be made of each student's contribution and their ability to work as part of a team or, sometimes, a group grade is given and each member of the group is given the same grade, according to how well the group performed. Areas of study where teamwork is important include some healthcare courses and theatre studies. In addition, some courses of professional education, such as teacher training, may include group work. Professionals work together on some tasks, and teachers also use group work with their pupils.

There are sound professional reasons for practising team work. In health care there may be interagency teams, in teaching there may be cross curricular projects, and theatre studies is focused on performances which, except for monologues, are team efforts.

There are many different kinds of groups and many reasons why people come together in groups, but those formed on HE courses will usually be given tasks to be performed and goals to be achieved. For example, depending on the course of study, the group may be asked to design an artefact or to plan an event or even to write and perform a short play.

There is a considerable literature on the nature of groups, group processes, group dynamics and the roles which members of groups tend to take on. Familiarise yourself with this literature if you feel that this would be helpful. (e.g. see Cottrell, 2003; Douglas, 2000; Tuckman and Jensen, 1977).

For group work to be successful, whilst keeping the group task in mind, you should recognise and respect the potential contributions and strengths of the other members of the group and use your own strengths to complement the strengths and weaknesses in the group as a whole. Rather than using your abilities to shine as an individual, you demonstrate your ability to help the group to successfully complete the task given. Working in groups, as with any other interpersonal interaction, requires flexibility, good observation of verbal and non-verbal clues, nuanced on-the-spot-judgements, and reflection in action.

The work of R.M. Belbin (2010) and his team focused on how management teams work and the team roles within them. They recognised the importance of making the most of individual team member's strengths and differences.

Successful groups, before they begin the group task, tend to clarify the purpose and aims of the group and the roles of team members, drawing on the knowledge and skills of those members. They approach the task systematically, rather than simply muddling through. Decisions will be made by the agreed leader, by democratic vote or by consensus. They will not be made by a minority or by default. There are different views about having a designated leader. For some groups, it may work well for members to take turns in taking on the role of leader. Again, there is literature on leadership (e.g. see Day, 1999). The leader is the most prominent member of the group, with the greatest influence and responsibility. Should you find yourself with this position, here are some of the elements that writers have identified as contributing to good leadership: vision, the ability to motivate the team, self-confidence and confidence in others, identification, drawing on and praising the individual contributions of the team to the team goal, being fair, polite and protective towards all team members, the ability to enthuse, the ability to delegate and to enable rather than control.

When a group is set up in an educational setting, if the students do not all know one another, it is useful to allow them to introduce themselves. This breaks the ice so that shy people will then find it easier to join in discussions.

Reviews

There are several kinds of review. Some involve looking over or surveying a particular area, as with a literature review and a research review. Others primarily involve critical discussion and evaluation, as with a book or a film or a play review. There are also more specialised reviews such as a literary review, involving interpretation of a text and drawing on literary theory.

We cannot cover the understanding and techniques required for a literary review since it would be impossible to cover all the learning involved for students in literature departments. Research reviews will be covered later, when we consider research projects. In this section, we will cover literature reviews and book reviews and a sample book review will be given.

Literature Reviews

You have learned in Chapter 1 how to identify the literature most relevant to your essay and you were advised to make notes on each book and paper. This is part of what you need to do in writing a literature review. Your assignment might involve reviewing the work of one writer. This would usually include all, or at least their major works. Or it might involve the most recent work on a particular topic, or the literature you think most significant for discussing a particular topic or answering a particular question. As set out in Chapter 1, you must identify the relevant literature and read critically and make notes.

Once you are sure you know what your tutor intends the task to be, and know the assessment criteria for it, you can plan your review. Your reader will need to be introduced to the range of relevant books and papers. You need to be concise and clear about the contents, level and the intended readership for each of these. What is distinctive about each? What are their strengths and weaknesses in relation to the essay question? What are your own well-supported opinions?

What is important for most such assignments is that you can demonstrate that you are familiar with and understand the most significant contributions to the literature about the subject under consideration. How inclusive you will need to be depends on the question asked. Some literature surveys, for example a survey of the work of a particular author, will usually need to be comprehensive. Other surveys will expect you to choose only the most worthwhile contributions. You will need to think deeply about what literature you select. Given the length of most assignments, you will probably need to be succinct. This entails that you learn how to pick out the most salient points and also convey the distinctive characteristics of each book or paper included.

Book Reviews

You may be asked to undertake a book review, possibly of a book on your recommended reading list. You must read the book carefully and critically; ensure that you understand each part of it. Think about the content, style and merit of the book. Who is it intended for and is it written at the appropriate level? What is its 'unique selling point' (USP)?

Mal was the review editor for many years for the *Journal of Moral Education*. She judged a review worthy of publication if it was written to the required length and such that the reader obtained a good and clear understanding of what the book was about. Other features, such as informed discussion of the central idea or a good critique of it were welcome. However, if after reading the review, one has no clear idea of the book's actual contents, the readers of the journal would not be able to judge if it was a book they might want to read. A clear and succinct outline of the contents can be followed by discussions and evaluations and disagreements, etc.

Your review task might have a special dimension. For example: *Review X for your fellow students. How useful will it be to them in relation to our proposed project?* Clearly, you will need to do your review with the project in mind and will need to answer the second part of the task. Or consider: *Choose the book which has been most useful to you in our work this term. Review this and say how it has been helpful to you.* Obviously, you will select a book that HAS been helpful to you. You will need to review this but also discuss its usefulness in relation to the term's studies.

Having taken account of any special aspects of the assignment, other things being equal, a good review will include: what the book is about, the intended readership, an indication of the contents, its particular slant, contributions or USP and some discussion of its strength and/or weaknesses. Depending on the length of the review – and this can vary from a brief few paragraphs to a full-scale essay-length piece of work – other possible inclusions are: background material (historical context or its place in the literature, etc.), comparison with another book or books, critical discussion of its contents and key ideas, your own considered and supported response (take care to be fair) and whether you would recommend it and why or why not.

Sample Reviews

The first review below is a brief, 500 word information review intended to allow students to judge whether the reviewed publication would be helpful to those seeking to improve their basic English.

The second review below is a copy of a review published in 1992. It reviews a well-written report and will lead us into the next section of this chapter on research reports and projects.

Sample Review: *Osmond, A. (2015) Academic Writing and Grammar for Students.*

'Meaningful, practical advice' is what Osmond intends this book to provide. The 'narrow focus' [sic] is on writing rather than on academic skills. The aim is to help students to get well-formed, clear sentences onto the page.

The eight chapters cover conventions of academic writing, the basic grammatical concepts, putting sentences together, putting paragraphs together, critical thinking

---

and referencing, conciseness and clarity, common mistakes and how to deal with them, and proofreading effectively. Apart from the brief chapter on critical thinking and referencing (14 pages) and a smaller number of sections on academic conventions such as using acronyms, avoiding the first and second person and presentation of tables and graphs, most of the book, as promised, is about writing good, basic English. Chapter 2 is particularly useful. It covers sentences and punctuation. Not forming proper sentences and incorrect punctuation are the most common characteristics of poor English. The final chapter is an appropriate ending, giving good advice about how to proofread effectively. Proofreading is quite a complex but very useful skill.

The book does not have long pages of uninterrupted prose. It is made accessible with boxed tutor comments, boxed key points and many examples. There is, however, a certain amount of repetition.

The book's strong point is that, unlike most other study skills guides for university students, it mostly keeps to the basics of good English, teaching about poor grammar, punctuation and how to improve clarity and style. Its weakness is that basic subjects are sometimes discussed in far from basic English. Paradoxically, it is sometimes written at a level which will be found difficult by some of the students, for example, dyslexic students and those learning English as a second language. (Suggestions about grammar books for second language learners are offered). Thus, in Chapter 2, an, arguably, unnecessary chapter on basic grammatical concepts, Osmond may be difficult to follow for some students:

> Both the second person singular and the second person plural are included for the sake of completeness. Verbs in the English language do not change if the second person is being used to address one person or a group (2015: 39)

and

> It is important to remember that the verbs you use must agree (that is, take the correct form) for the noun or nouns you are using. Some nouns are singular, but refer to a collection of multiple things. (2015: 36)

However, most chapters provide clear help for the many students who, though literate, need to brush up on their basic English. Students can use the sections about grammar, punctuation and style and ignore parts of the book which are less helpful. The sections on critical thinking, for example, are too brief to do justice to this complex subject and are a separate issue from 'practical advice' with a 'narrow' focus. Nevertheless, this is a book that can be recommended to those students whose academic work is pulled down by poor English.

(487 Words)

Sample Review: *Bourne, J. (1989): Moving into the Mainstream: LEA Provision for Bilingual Pupils. Windsor: NFER Nelson.*

This book reports the findings of the Bilingual Pupils Project (1985–88), carried out by the National Foundation for Educational Research. The survey was thorough and timely – obtaining responses from 80% of education authorities (and including detailed studies of seven) about their English as a second language and community languages teaching and support. Thus, in the mid-eighties, just prior to a time of educational change, we are given a picture of national provision for bilingual pupils against which the impact of the 1988 Education Bill can be evaluated in future research.

Following current educational usage, the author defines bilingual as a pupil who uses more than one language in his/her daily life, outside the formal modern language learning classroom. She recognises both that many bilingual pupils may be multilingual and the highly political nature of provision.

In the introduction the policy context is analysed, within an historical perspective, and details given of language surveys in England and Wales. She concludes that in talking about bilingual pupils one is not talking about exceptional cases in a few urban authorities, but about a substantial proportion of the school population. The implications of this bilingual presence need to be clearly considered in national policy making, and in the national curriculum. The second chapter explores Extra Staff and Special Funding. The survey revealed uncertainty over the future use of Section II funding with a consensus that extra funds were required to meet the needs of minority ethnic groups. A pluralist perspective was making some impact on provision for bilingual pupils but there was little LEA encouragement of minority group participation in decision making and policy formation.

The next three chapters deal with the use of extra staffing for English Language support, bilingual support and community language teaching. Most LEAs had a policy of supporting bilingual pupils in the mainstream class, with very different perceptions of what this means in practice. Over a third of LEAs in England were making provision for community languages – on the whole, bilingual support in the primary school and community language support in the secondary, with some financial support to linguistic minority organisations for voluntary language classes. Numbers of community language staff were low in comparison to number of English language support staff. Recruitment of community language staff was being hampered by difficulties in obtaining qualified teacher status for experienced bilingual teachers and by LEAs inability to claim Section II funding for instructors undertaking training on secondment. There are about 500,000 Welsh speakers in Wales and considerable experience of bilingual provision in Welsh schools. The author provides a chapter on Welsh Language Education. In contrast to the Swann Report (DES, 1985) this project report claims that analysis of bilingual education in Wales raises useful political and practical questions for the English context: about the possibility of developing bilingual provision in England parallel to monolingual English education, as in Wales; about the desirability of teaching local community languages to monolingual pupils and teachers, as in Wales, if a multilingual society is to be created; and, if attempting to provide for other languages within a common curriculum and integrated classroom, how to ensure continuity and progression in the bilingual programmes on offer, so that the introduction of other languages (whether first or second languages) can be of real educational value to pupils.

This survey found some provision for bilingual pupils, and LEA readiness to develop this provided a central policy lead and support was made available. Unfortunately, real constraints on this development were also found: the absence of consultation structures, of funding to support training for bilingual teachers, of clearly marked national in-service priority funding (GRIST) and of any central curriculum and materials development body for bilingualism. Unsurprisingly, then, Jill Bourne concluded that the indications are that future policy will not be based on a pluralist perspective but on the assumption that the new national curriculum will somehow be culturally neutral – overlooking linguistic and cultural diversity and unprepared to address discrimination within the system itself. She advocates a more educational development of the knowledge about languages that children already have. There is much to be learnt about language and society from adopting a bilingual perspective.

This is a well written and competent book. The author successfully conveys the impact of complex issues on bilingual provision, including Section II funding mechanisms and other constraints on progressive developments. She fulfils her stated aim of providing information on policy and provision, in England and Wales in the mid-1980s, to those concerned with the education of bilingual pupils: LEA officers, teachers, teacher trainers, community organizations, parents and policy makers.

Writing Reports

You may be given a report to write for one of your assignments. The report could be of an event, for example a day conference, or of a survey, or of your module and so on. Unlike a review, your main task is to provide a clear, comprehensive account rather than an evaluation. However, this is only a matter of main intention. A good review will convey clear information about the object under review as well as evaluation, and a good report will convey some evaluation of that which is reviewed as well as being, primarily, a clear account of it.

Because your report brief can take any number of forms you should check with your tutor about the format, length, voice, style and any particular requirements. The following section offers general guidelines, but these do not take precedence over any guidelines you may be given.

Format

Reports usually have a standard format which includes an executive summary, an introduction or background section, methodology, the body of the report itself, and conclusions and recommendations. Check with your department or tutor the report section format required as well as the length of the report. Also check whether you will gain any additional marks for the inclusion of tables, charts and graphs and if so, then spend time incorporating these into the document and presenting them well.

Within this standard format, and depending on the purpose of the report, there may be some variations to the standard format. Other considerations will be the depth of analysis required, and the subject or discipline. For example, a financial report that you might produce for a business studies course will be different from the report format for a science based topic or an arts or humanities topic.

Most reports are presented with headings and subheadings. Headings should be in a larger font than subheadings. Be sure to be consistent. Your headings and subheadings should organise your report in a logical way.

Style

Most reports will be written in a clear, formal style and in an impersonal voice with an objective tone. Imagine you are writing to inform an intelligent reader who does not have full knowledge about the topic of the report. Be unambiguous, with direct, non-metaphorical sentences.

Presentation

All the academic rules, such as the use of acronyms and referencing etc. apply.

Competent Reports

Now consider the second review above. This is a good review of what was clearly a competent report. As a good review it provides clear information about the contents of the report, including useful background information and the negative and positive findings of the survey being reported. It draws justified conclusions and makes sensible recommendations and finishes with a fair evaluation of the report.

The report being reviewed is a report of the findings of a large survey of education authorities on their second language teaching and support. It was clearly a well-structured and informative report. It gives 'a picture of national provision for bilingual pupils against which the impact of the 1988 Education Bill can be evaluated in future research'. It begins with key definitions and the highly political background. It goes on to give clear outlines of the key elements of the survey and concludes with some well-considered implications and conclusions. The author of the report, Jill Bourne, succeeds in conveying the complex issues of the survey.

There are useful lessons here for writing a competent report, should this be asked of you as an assignment.

1. As with Bourne's report, give information in your introductory paragraph about the document, project or event which you are reporting.
2. Also in the introductory section include definitions, if these would be useful, and relevant, useful background information e.g. the local, national, historical or political context.
3. In the body of your report identify, explain and discuss all the key elements.
4. In the concluding section you could provide a summary of the key points, recommendations and an evaluation of the strengths and weaknesses of your subject. You could also, relatively briefly, give your own point of view.

Research Projects

You may be asked to write a report of a piece of research which was conducted by yourself or by others. This will be a relatively long report – 7,000 words or more. You will need to include an introduction, a literature review, a discussion of methodology, the presentation, analysis and discussion of the findings (their contributions and limitations) and a conclusion with summary and recommendations.

A dissertation with, say, 10,000 or more words, may additionally require background information, a theoretical framework and a discussion of ethical and epistemological issues. For such a sustained research project and report you will need some further tutor guidance, reading and research training. We would recommend: Bell (2005) and Cohen, Manion and Morrison (2000).

The structure and format of your research project will largely be determined by the discipline you are writing for. Is the report for your business studies course, for a humanities project or is it a scientific report? You will need to follow the academic conventions for each of these fields. A scientific paper, for example, will often include tables, figures and charts based on some form of statistical analysis, and there will be specific formats required for these. A business studies report will follow the academic conventions that are accepted in the commercial world and may include research requiring market and competitor analysis, which are often presented in tables and chart format.

As with all the advice you have been given throughout this book, it is always wise to check what is required for this particular piece of work in your academic institution and follow the guidelines given. If you have any doubts, discuss the requirements with your tutor.

Other Forms of Writing

Reflective Journals

On some courses students may be required to keep a journal. You should check if this is to be assessed. If so, find out the learning outcomes intended and the marking criteria to be used. Plan and write accordingly.

If the journal covers your experience of the whole module, keep notes and spend some time on relevant reading and first draft writing as you go. In other words, do not leave creating your journal from scratch to the end of the year. The advice given on pages 87–89 about metacognition and reflections on your own thinking and learning may be helpful for aspects of your journal.

A reflective journal is a personal log, and while there may be some guidelines and advice on the format to be used, how you keep your journal will largely be a personal preference. However, sometimes the reflective journal will be assessed as part of the marking criteria, and you need to be aware of this so that you present your journal in a way that will help you to achieve a higher grade. Some students like to keep a reflective journal in a diary format where they write notes up at regular intervals and record what has taken place followed by notes on their reflection on this. Others use audio or video recording tools.

The main purpose of a reflective journal is to help you to develop your own knowledge and skills through a process of questioning, critical thinking and reflection. This is designed to support your experiential learning and practice. To this end, your journal will be used to focus on a key area or question within your work, and you will then need to think about and document events that have happened, what was said and by whom, how this made you feel and what your own thoughts were at the time. You may also record what you thought and felt about other people's thoughts, feelings, emotions, moods, body language, etc., which will provide additional layers of information that may lead to insights. (If you are writing about other people, remember to keep the information confidential by referring to them as Mr X or Mrs Y, for example.)

There are a number of professions that use reflective practice as a key part of different roles. For example, education, teaching and health care. Other roles where both personal and professional development are a key aspect also use reflective practice (architects, human resources professionals, journalists, etc.).

A course of study is a personal journey so even if you are not required to keep a journal, it may be a good idea to do so for a number of reasons. It will allow you to look back and see your achievements as they have unfolded. You will be able to see how your thinking and other skills have developed. You will be able to see where you have arrived at particular insights or roadblocks along the way and last but not least it gets you into good practice for writing. Some students use their journal as a way of 'warming up' before they move on to the work of writing their essay or assignment.

Abstracts and Summaries

Many students find writing short abstracts or summaries quite difficult. The knack is being able to pick out the most salient points. Write these down in clear, short sentences. They should be the bones or skeleton of the longer piece being summarised. Do not include subsidiary themes, anecdotes, examples, etc.

The sentences you have written down form the basis of your abstract. Have you missed out anything important? Add another sentence. Do any of the sentences require more explanation? Add this in as succinctly as possible.

When you have completed your abstract, do a word count and adjust wordage as necessary. See page 105 for advice on doing this.

You should now have a piece with approximately the correct number of words. This usually means within 10% of the word allowance. For example, for a 500 word allowance you must produce not fewer than 450 and not more than 550 words.

Your aim is to produce, in clear and unambiguous English, an accurate overview of the longer piece. It will be an accurate overview if it covers all the main aspects. A summary must omit a detailed account of the main points while creating a comprehensible statement of them. You reproduce the key content of the original.

Portfolios

Some courses require students to produce a portfolio of work, which is often in support of a practical piece of work or where a student is being assessed during a work placement. Often vocational courses will use portfolios as a way of assessing student learning. Portfolios may be produced in a variety of formats, but will often require written analysis and reporting of both processes and findings undertaken in practical work as well as learning objectives and outcomes. You may also be required to take photographs of the work being produced and annotate this to show that you have understood the tasks.

Depending on the type of course you are taking, the marking criteria for portfolios may carry significant weighting.

Negative and Positive Approaches

Chapter 8 has considered non-essay, written forms of assignment including group work, reviews, reports, summaries/abstracts, portfolios and journals. Always check with your tutor what is expected for a particular assignment and make sure you understand the marking criteria. Without this knowledge you may well find you receive comments such as:

Negative Comments

- Your report misses out the main message of the book.
- You deal with the morning lectures of the conference, but say nothing about the workshops in the afternoon. You could have said what these were and given an overview of the one you chose to attend.
- Your review gives a good, clear account of the contents of the book, but no indication of your own evaluation.
- Your piece falls well short of the word allowance. Small wonder that much is omitted and that there is little critical comment.

Once you are clear about specific requirements for this particular assignment, you can consider the general nature of the assignment. For instance, reviews will usually contain some evaluative material, reports will usually be accurate and clear and abstract/summaries must concisely cover all the main points. This preparatory understanding should help you to achieve comments such as:

Positive Comments

- Your review gives the reader a clear idea of what the book is about and why you would recommend it to philosophy students. Well done.
- Your report in the first part of the essay is accurately and clearly written. You give equal attention to the reflective part two. A competent piece of work.
- Your abstract clearly and accurately covers all the main contents of the essay. To write clearly and concisely is a useful skill.
- Your literature review is comprehensive. You include all the most important books and papers and demonstrate that you understand why these are relevant.

Brief Exercise: Evaluate Two Reviews

Read two book reviews in a quality newspaper. Were they helpful/informative/interesting? Why? Why not?

Helpful advice is given in Appendix 4.

Conclusion

As was pointed out at the start of this chapter, do not neglect the advice of the first seven chapters of this book. All your assignments, including non-essay forms, must follow this advice in order to obtain a good grade for HE level work. However, additionally, for non-essay assignments consider the following:

- **Purpose**
  For example, a review usually seeks to survey and evaluate its subject by combining an accurate, informative account of it with a sense of its merits and drawbacks. A report usually seeks to convey the main substance of its subject.
- **Format**
  There are different report formats so be sure that you are following what is required by your tutor.
- **Marking criteria**
  Always check the marking criteria for your non-essay assignments. Be aware if there is any weighting of the marks for various aspects of the work.
- **Tutor expectations**
  For these non-essay assignments, it is particularly important that you understand what your tutor is expecting.

By being clear about what is expected of you for a particular form of assignment and for a particular instance of this form of assignment you will be better able to obtain that high grade.

Summary of Key Points

For non-essay assignments, as with essays, you need to follow the advice in this book about reading the literature; demonstrating this reading; planning your work; being rational, critical and analytical; presenting your work in a professional manner and using the correct academic conventions. However, you also need to know the additional requirements of non-essay assignments. Check the marking criteria for the assignment and discuss with your tutor what is expected.

1. Group work

    - Your own contribution to the group work task and your group work skills may be assessed individually or you may receive a group grade.
    - Working in groups requires flexibility, observation of verbal and non-verbal clues, nuanced on the spot judgement and reflection-in-action.
    - Successful groups clarify the purpose and aims of the group and the roles of group members, drawing on their knowledge and skills.
    - Such groups work systematically.
    - If a leader would be useful, check out the characteristics of an effective leader on page 122.

2. Reviews

    Literature and research reviews

    - Literature reviews and research reviews require a survey of a particular area. There are relevant suggestions in Chapters 1 and 3 and advice on longer research projects in this chapter.
    - You must show that you understand the most significant contributions in the literature about the subject under review.
    - Pick out the significant points for each book or paper included.

    Book and film reviews

    - A book or film review will involve critical discussion and evaluation.
    - First read the book carefully and critically.
    - Think about the content, style and merits of the book.
    - Who is the book intended for? Is it written at the appropriate level?
    - What is its unique selling point (USP)?
    - Write to the required length but include a clear account of the contents of the book, followed by discussion and evaluation.
    - Good reviews will usually include: what the book is about, its intended readership, contents, USP, strengths and weaknesses.
    - Longer reviews could also cover: background material, comparison with another book or books, critical discussion of the key ideas, your own response (taking care to be fair) and whether you would recommend it.

3.   Reports

- The main task is to give a clear and comprehensive account of that which is being reported.
- Check with your tutor about the format, length, style and particular requirements for your report.
- Reports usually require an executive summary, an introduction or background section, methodology if a research report, the body of the report itself, and conclusions and recommendations.
- Use a clear, formal style and an impersonal (passive) voice.
- Be unambiguous with direct, non-metaphorical sentences.

4.   Reflective journal

- Check whether your journal will be assessed and if so check the marking criteria and write accordingly.
- The advice on page 87 about metacognition – reflection on your own thinking/ learning – may be useful.
- Document relevant events, conversations, emotions at the time.
- When you write about others keep the information confidential by, for example, referring to them as Mr X or Ms Y.

5.   Abstracts and summaries

- Pick out the most crucial points. These are the bones of your abstract.
- Do not include subsidiary themes, anecdotes or examples.
- Your aim is to provide a clear overview of the main content of the original.

6.   Portfolios

- If you are required to keep a portfolio of work you may need to include written analysis, reporting of processes, findings of practical work, annotated photographs and other supportive and explanatory material.
- Check what format your portfolio of work should take, what it should include and the marking criteria and weighting.

Top Tip – it is impossible to cover every kind of assignment which students might be given on all the variety of courses and modules. Our top tip, therefore, is to be clear about what your tutor wants and expects, and to be aware of any guidelines, learning outcomes and marking criteria. If possible, read one or two good examples of the kind of assignment you have been given.

For chapter exercise feedback, further reading ideas and more tips on polishing your assignment, check out the appendices at the back of the book.

References

Belbin, R.M. (2010) *Team Roles at Work* (2nd edition). Abingdon: Routledge.

Bell, J. (2005) *Doing Your Research Project: A Guide for First Time Researchers in Education, Health and Social Science* (4th edition). Maidenhead: Open University Press.

Bourne, J. (1989) *Moving into Mainstream. LEA Provision for Bilingual Pupils.* Windsor: NFER-Nelson.

Cohen, L., Manion, L. and Morrison, K. (2000) *Research Methods in Education.* London: Routledge.

Cottrell, S. (2003) *The Study Skills Handbook* (2nd edition). Basingstoke: Palgrave Macmillan.

Day, C. (1999) *Developing Teachers: The Challenges of Lifelong Learning.* London: Routledge.

DES (1985) *The Swann Report.* London: DfEE

Douglas, T. (2000) *Basic Groupwork* (2nd edition). Abingdon: Routledge.

Osmond, A. (2015) *Academic Writing and Grammar for Students* (2nd edition). London: Sage.

Tuckman, B.W. and Jensen, M.A.C. (1977) 'Stages of small group development revisited', *Group and Organizational Studies*, 2: 419–27.

9

Oral Assignments: Lectures and Short Talks

Overview

- Introduction
- Gain Self-Confidence
- Engage Your Audience
- Structure Your Talk
- Short Talks Without PowerPoint
- PowerPoint Presentations
- Negative and Positive Approaches
- Conclusion
- Summary of Key Points
- References

Introduction

You may be asked to make an oral presentation to your fellow students about some aspect of the course. This may be because you have a particular interest in this area. Or it may be that, as a pedagogic device, your tutor likes to involve all students in learning through such presentations. The presenter and the audience can learn from each of their presentations.

Presentations may be 15 minute short talks, or say, a 40 minute session involving 20 minutes of presentation and 20 minutes answering questions about it. Sometimes, these oral presentations constitute graded assignments. Ask your tutor if this is the case and, if so, find out the marking criteria being used. Whatever the length of the presentation, and whether it is graded or not, in this chapter we will focus on how you can give a good talk/lecture.

Gain Self-Confidence

Almost everyone is nervous about giving a talk. Indeed, it is said that a little nervousness may give an edge to your performance. However, the more self-confidence you can summon, the more effective you are likely to be. You will then be seen to be in control of your material, and knowledgeable but not arrogant.

Your self-confidence will increase if you know that you have put time and effort into preparing your presentation. This preparation should include practising delivering your talk. Preparation includes rehearsal. Rehearse firstly for yourself and then to a friend or friends. You will then discover if the timing is right. If your talk is longer than it should be you must judge what to cut out. If it is too short, then what that is of relevance and interest could you add? You may get feedback from your small audience. More importantly, you will get a sense of which parts of the presentation work well and which parts are unclear or drag, or need examples, etc.

Engage Your Audience

The more interested you are yourself in the subject of your presentation the more likely it is that you will engage your audience. You are likely to have some choice over your topic, so choose wisely and find a topic or an element of a topic that genuinely holds some fascination for you.

As well as giving thought to the subject matter of your lecture, consider your audience, too. Your presentation should be pitched at the right level. You must not patronise your audience, but you must not overwhelm them with too much detail either. Most of us cannot absorb a stream of new material. A small number of key points, well illustrated, perhaps with the occasional personal illustrative short anecdote, will be listened to with more pleasure and more learning will take place than with an over-packed stream of facts and figures. (See the note on personal anecdotes on page 96.) Practise your 'reflection-in-action' by monitoring the audience reaction and have some modifications of your material prepared, in case these are required.

It is easy to let your nervousness make you play safe, not daring to make a joke or include a personal example or a new idea. While it would be a mistake for an inexperienced lecturer to have a constant stream of experimental material, you can afford to include some less safe elements. One flat joke is not a disaster.

Structure Your Talk

In structuring your talk, seek some variety in your material and its presentation. This will keep the audience interested. Thus, for example, you might follow a rather abstract explanation of the key idea with a short anecdote about the thinker or with some relevant practical applications that the idea has generated.

In thinking about structure, take account of the advice in Chapter 2. For example, begin with an appropriate, perhaps attention-grabbing introduction, follow with a logical development and end with a satisfying conclusion.

Short Talks Without PowerPoint

As we have indicated, each student may be asked to give a short talk to the rest of the group on some aspect of the module. If you must only talk for, say, 15 minutes, a PowerPoint presentation is probably not expected.

Choose your topic carefully. It must be a topic able to be covered in a short talk and it must be of interest to the group. Think about the lectures or seminars and discussions which everyone found interesting. Make notes on these. Make a plan of what you want to say. Take keywords that will guide you through your plan. These keywords can be written on a card that you can glance at to prompt you.

You want to grab attention in your opening, and continue with varied content to a satisfying conclusion. By 'vary' we mean, for example, that you can move from, say, an abstract definition to a concrete example to a brief but interesting anecdote.

The sample prompt card is for a topic on Eysenck's personality traits and criminality, chosen by a student taking a module on criminality who had noticed that the lectures on personality traits had caught everyone's attention. By limiting her talk to one account of personality traits, the talk could be successfully restricted to 15 minutes.

```
┌─────────────────┤ Sample Plan for Short Talk ├─────────────────┐
```

Introduction

Focused on the interesting notion of personality traits (PT); for the students on our course the possible link with criminal behaviour is fascinating.

Personality trait – an individual's personality is made up of traits which can have important implications for their behaviour.

It has been claimed that criminal behaviour can be explained by the link between personality traits and a propensity to this behaviour.

Focused on Eysenck's account because he was the first to develop an account of personality traits and his work has been influential for psychologists.

Main Part: Explore the idea of a link

- Explain Eysenck's account.

'PT' – biologically inherited differences

Three main PTs as basis for variations in behaviour:

1. Extrovert/introvert – sociability/impulsive/lively
2. Neuroticism/Socialisation – tendency for recklessness, hostility, anger
3. Psychoticism/Stability – emotional stability

Do these link with criminal behaviour? The theory predicts that criminal behaviour links with extroverted, neurotic and psychotic and not so much with introverted, socialised, stable (Putwain and Sammons, 2002).

Explain the studies which agree that there is such a link (Harkins, 1975).

Explain the studies that have major criticisms of the suggested link, e.g. Studies only included males, (Hayes, 2000); mostly based on self-report questionnaires which may be unreliable, there may be a link with the impulsiveness of the extrovert but not with sociability (Putwain and Sammons, 2002).

Conclusion

Mixed Findings

Both PTs and criminality are too complex for a predictive link to be fully explained by any one theory. Human beings are too complex for their behaviour to be explained by any one theory. However, some theories, including Eysenck's account of PTs, add to our understanding of criminal behaviour.

Interesting topic

Define "personality trait"

The claim

Why choose Eysenck?

Main Part

1. Explain Eysenck's account

2. Explain the studies that agree with the putative link

3. Explain the studies that criticise the link

Conclusion

Mixed findings but some significant findings and useful ideas

Give my own view

FIGURE 9.1   Sample short talk prompt card

PowerPoint Presentations

For a long lecture, as distinct from a short talk, it may help you to do a PowerPoint presentation. This helps the audience to follow the main points and to stay with you. The PowerPoint slides also help you to avoid leaving out chunks of your intended material or scrambling to regain the sequence you intended to follow.

Do not try to cram all your lecture on to PowerPoint slides. This is pointless. As you and they read it together, the audience will be bored and they will rightly wonder why you need to be there at all. The points on the PowerPoint slides are key pegs upon which you will hang your much fuller presentation. You may even choose to use images to convey your key points. You explain, expand on, discuss and illustrate these pegs. Similarly, the notes to accompany the slides remind you of how to expand on the PowerPoint pegs. They, too, are not meant to be read aloud. They are a memory aid which only you will see. They prompt you on the key aspects to expand on and elaborate as you deliver your lecture.

The sample PowerPoint presentation provided includes jokes in brackets. For some presenters and some audiences these would be useful. An inexperienced lecturer may prefer not to include jokes and for some more formal occasions they would not be appropriate.

This PowerPoint presentation also includes points, particularly for slides 7 and 8, where the audience may be invited to participate. Audience participation

141

can help the lecturer to hold the audience interest and the audience are more likely to remember the content. Again this device may not always be appropriate, for example, if you do not feel you could handle this confidently or if there would not be time.

To sum up, in what follows we show your (i.e. the lecturer's) thoughts pruned down to the prompt notes you will use. And these prompt notes are followed by the relevant accompanying PowerPoint slide.

Sample PowerPoint Presentation

The sample PowerPoint presentation is for a lecture entitled: What is Philosophy? The prompt notes, which only you (the lecturer) see, come first, with the slide which your audience will see following. You could have your prompt notes on an A6 card or in the 'notes' section of your PowerPoint software.

Do not worry if the notes shown are too concise for you to make sense of. They were for the sole use of the presenter who wrote them. This is only a sample to show you how a PowerPoint works. It is not an attempt to teach you about philosophy. The sample could have been on any topic. For a PowerPoint which you prepare, your prompt notes will make sense to you and should be sufficient to allow you to talk through each of the PowerPoint slides which you have prepared. In other words, the sample is intended to show you how brief 'aide memoire' notes can help you to expand on and explain PowerPoint slides to produce a good lecture.

At the start of your lecture, you can indicate the structure of the session. About how long will the lecture be? Will there be time for questions? Will there be a break before the questions? You could let your audience know if you prefer questions at the end or are happy to take them as you go. You could indicate what your presentation will cover and what you hope they will gain from it. Think about what initial information would be useful to this particular audience.

Your first slide gives the title of the presentation. In the sample PowerPoint the presenter will attempt to introduce the notion of philosophy – they will attempt to throw some light on a complex subject.

Lecture prompt notes: *Slide 1: What is Philosophy?*

The structure of the session

What will be covered

The nature of the question

The lecture title; not an empirical question

What is Philosophy?

A philosophical question!

Lecture prompt notes: *Slide 2: Two Laws*

Read the two laws

Explain the point [i.e. there are no right or wrong answers to philosophical questions]

The right questions

Traditional philosophical questions

With increased human knowledge, some of these questions become a matter for science. For example, the once debated question about whether colour is a primary property of objects has been understood in terms of light waves, which have been discovered scientifically.

What is Philosophy?

A philosophical question!

The First Law of Philosophy:

"For every philosopher, there is an equal and opposite philosopher"

The Second Law of Philosophy:

"They are both wrong"

Key Point: Philosophical questions cannot be answered scientifically (empirically) i.e. by observation and experiment

(Continued)

(Continued)

Lecture prompt notes: *Slide 3: Substantive and Analytic Philosophy*

Substantive philosophy – explain with examples

Substantive moral philosophy – explain with examples

Analytic philosophy – explain with examples

Analytic moral philosophy – explain with examples

What is Philosophy?

Substantive — and — Analytic Philosophy:

A philosophy of life
+
Moral questions

Analysis through critical
reflection
+
Ethics

Lecture prompt notes: *Slide 4: Reflection*

Conceptual analysis – explain with examples

Socratic dialogue – explain with examples

Critical thinking – explain with examples

Meta-analysis – explain with examples

What is Analytic Reflection?

Conceptual Analysis
Socratic Dialogue
Critical Thinking
Meta-analysis

I think therefore I am single

Lecture prompt notes: *Slide 5: Family Resemblance Concepts*

Explain 'family resemblance concept'

Explain the chart

Wittgenstein's Family Resemblance Concept

Can engineering approaches, methods or models help philosophers to "look and see"; to uncover the "family resemblances" across uses of a word in a complex, dynamic variety of contexts?

	Rule Following	Recreational	Skilful	Competitive	Physical Exercise
Professional Football	✔		✔	✔	✔
Chess	✔	✔	✔	✔	
Solitaire (cards)	✔	✔			
Child's make believe game			✔		✔

Lecture prompt notes: *Slide 6: Branches of Philosophy*

Explain:

Epistemology

Ethics

Metaphysics

Ontology

All 'philosophy of' areas have non empirical questions relevant to that area – give examples

What is Philosophy?

Branches of philosophy

Epistemology	(Theory of Knowledge)
Ethics	(Normative and Meta-ethics)
Metaphysics	
Ontology	

Philosophy of
- Education
- Science
- Religion
- Art (Aesthetics)
- Engineering
- Philosophy of Mind
- Philosophy of Language

(Continued)

(Continued)

Lecture prompt notes: *Slide 7: Branches of Philosophy: Examples of questions*

Read the questions as given and explain these.

If there is time and if it seems appropriate for this audience, ask them for suggestions of questions appropriate to each of these four areas.

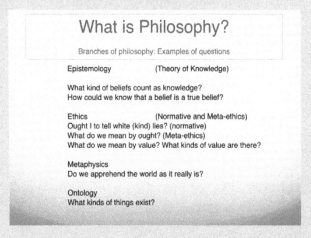

What is Philosophy?

Branches of philosophy: Examples of questions

Epistemology   (Theory of Knowledge)

What kind of beliefs count as knowledge?
How could we know that a belief is a true belief?

Ethics   (Normative and Meta-ethics)
Ought I to tell white (kind) lies? (normative)
What do we mean by ought? (Meta-ethics)
What do we mean by value? What kinds of value are there?

Metaphysics
Do we apprehend the world as it really is?

Ontology
What kinds of things exist?

Lecture prompt notes: *Slide 8: More Branches of Philosophy: Examples of questions*

Again go through the sample questions on the chart and explain these a little more.

If there is time and if it seems appropriate to this audience, ask for suggestions for further questions which fit with each area.

What is Philosophy?

More branches of philosophy: Examples of questions

Philosophy of
- Education – What is the difference between education and indoctrination? What do we mean by learning?
- Science – Are successive generations of scientists getting nearer to the truth about the world?
- Religion – Does God exist? – What kinds of evidence would justify a claim that God exists?
- Art (Aesthetics) - What do we mean by beauty?
- Engineering – What is the difference between engineering and technology?
- Mind – Do minds exist? What is the relationship between mind and brain?
- Language – What is meaning? What is the relationship between words and the world?

Lecture prompt notes: *Slide 9: So, What is Philosophy?*

Conclusion of the lecture. Some of the key points explaining the nature of philosophy and philosophical questions.

Emphasis on non empirical

The feeling of wonder

Philosophy is 'queen of the sciences' – explain

Finally, end with the fascination of philosophy

So,
what is philosophy?

Negative and Positive Approaches

In Chapter 9, we have considered how you can approach oral assignments such as short talks or longer presentations/lectures. Prepare your talk or lecture and practise giving it (to yourself and to friends or a relative). Without preparation and practice, you are unlikely to give an interesting and informative talk, delivered with confidence, and may well receive comments such as:

Negative Comments

- The content of your presentation was of good quality. It was well researched and well explained. Unfortunately, your delivery was poor. You mumbled and could often not be heard.
- Your delivery of your presentation was very flat and monotonous. Try to be more lively.
- Your lecture was entertaining, particularly the jokes and anecdotes. However it was rather thin in content. We learned very little about your subject.
- Your PowerPoint slides were badly presented and seemed to have little connection to what you were saying.

147

If you prepare and practise, you will improve your talk. In preparation, just as with an essay, you need to have done some reading and some planning. To hold your audience's interest, it helps to have produced some fresh (original) material. In addition, you must consider the level and expectations of your audience, and to keep their attention, especially in a longer talk or lecture, to vary the content. A lecture may also benefit from the use of a PowerPoint presentation.

To monitor your audience and adjust accordingly (reflection-in-action) will require confidence, but is a bonus. However, simple preparation and practice will help you to achieve a better grade and feedback such as:

Positive Comments

- You gave a good lecture. The content was interesting and your delivery was clear and engaging. Well done.
- You explained difficult material very clearly and with interesting and helpful examples.
- Your lecture was informative, well delivered and engaged our interest. You dealt with the question and answer session very well. You answered each question competently, clearly and pleasantly, ensuring that the questioner felt that they had asked a good question.
- Your PowerPoint presentation was excellent. Your slides were well presented, clear and helpful. They added to your good presentation of a well-organised, well-researched and interesting lecture on a well-chosen topic.

Brief Exercise: Take a Critical Stance

Next time you listen to a lecture, notice which parts kept your attention. Why? What did you remember later?

Feedback is given in Appendix 4.

Conclusion

If you are asked to give an (assessed) oral presentation, your delivery, as well as the content or substance of the lecture, will influence the assessor. You must practise the delivery in advance as part of your preparation. Match your delivery to the occasion and your content to your audience. Ask your tutor what is expected in terms of audience participation and questions. If PowerPoint is permitted, take advantage of this. PowerPoint will help you to deliver all the material you intended, in the order you planned. It will also help you to feel confident and supported.

Summary of Key Points

1. If you have to give a short talk or a longer lecture as part of your module, find out if it will be given a grade. If so, what are the marking criteria? Plan accordingly.
2. Check if audience participation is allowed (or even expected). Such participation often helps to hold audience attention, increasing their enjoyment and their retention of what you have told them.
3. You must prepare and rehearse your talk/lecture.
4. Knowing you have put time and effort into preparing your presentation and that you have practised delivering it will give you confidence. Speak as clearly as you can.
5. By rehearsing and delivering your talk you will discover if your timing is correct, or if the length needs adjustment.
6. If you can choose your topic, choose a subject you genuinely find interesting. This will come across.
7. Consider your audience. Select material likely to be of interest to them and pitch it at an appropriate level.
8. A small number of key points, well illustrated, perhaps varied with the occasional brief anecdote, will keep interest and attention more than a stream of unrelieved facts and figures.
9. Begin with an interesting introduction, followed by a logical development and end with a satisfying conclusion.
10. For a lecture, as distinct from a short talk, a PowerPoint presentation may be helpful.
11. The memory aid for a short talk, where a PowerPoint presentation may be overkill, could be a small card which reminds you of the structure of your talk and gives you the key points you will speak to. (See the example given in this chapter.)
12. The points in the PowerPoint slides are brief pegs on which to hang your lecture – they should not be the whole lecture verbatim. You explain, expand on, discuss and illustrate these pegs. (See the example given in this chapter.)

For chapter exercise feedback, further reading ideas and more tips on polishing your assignment, check out the appendices following this chapter.

References

Harkins, S. and Green, R.G. (1975) 'Discriminability and criterion differences between extrovert and introvert during vigilance', *Journal of Research in Personality*, 9 (4): 335–40.
Hayes, N. (2000) *Foundations of Psychology* (3rd edition). London: Thomson Learning.
Putwain, D. and Sammons, A. (2002) *Psychology and Crime*. Hove: Routledge.

Appendices

Appendix 1
Checklists

Checklist One

After you have finished your essay or assignment, use this checklist to ensure your best work.

1. Title

Is the title at the top of your work the correct one (if you were given a title), and is it accurately worded (if you picked your own topic)?
   Does your answer fit this title and cover all parts?

2. Macro check

Read your work to check that the content is relevant, demonstrates your knowledge of the literature, is well organised, contains some critical material and some of your own ideas or point of view.
   Does the essay have too much repetition or any glaring omissions?

3. Micro check

Read your work to check presentation, spelling, punctuation and grammar. Have you made good use of paragraphs? Have you presented acronyms, quotations, tables and charts and references correctly?
   It is actually quite difficult to proofread for small errors because you get drawn into the meaning, the macro elements. Some people suggest reading your work backwards, i.e. from the last sentence upwards so that you are focused on what is on the page, the actual sentences, rather than the overall meaning.

For the Final Checks

Read your essay out loud. This may draw your attention to something you missed when simply reading.

Read the essay or assignment a final time. Imagine you are the assessor as you read. Is everything clearly worded? Is there anything you could improve, cut, add to, amend, change, explain?

Checklist Two

The following checklist is based on the advice of the chapters you have read and thus covers the main characteristics of an essay that should achieve a high grade in higher education.

1. **The Literature:** Have you made a balanced use of relevant literature?
2. **Planning:** Have you made and followed a well-structured plan? Does the essay have too much repetition or any glaring omissions?
3. **Rationality (reasons, evidence and argument):** Have you supported, and not merely asserted, your claims?
4. **Critical Thinking:** Have you demonstrated critical thinking?
5. **Analysis:** And/or have you used some meta-analysis?
6. **Originality:** Have you included an element original to you?
7. **Presentation:** Is your essay clearly printed, written in good English and spellchecked? Have you used paragraphs well? Have you produced accurate acronyms, quotations, tables and charts and references in accordance with the accepted academic conventions?
8. **Other Forms of Assignment:** Have you written your non-essay form of assignment with its particular requirements in mind?
9. **Oral Assignments:** For talks and lectures, have you rehearsed to check your timing and to practise your delivery?

Appendix 2
Punctuation

Colon

Use before a quote or a list.
   e.g. Explain what the following acronyms stand for: HE, WEA, FE, ESL, SEN.

Semicolon

Whereas you use a comma in a simple list, you use a semicolon in a complex list.

e.g. Comma

Brookfield identified four aspects of critical thinking as identifying assumptions, recognising the importance of context, imagining alternatives and reflective scepticism.

e.g. Semicolon

Brookfield identified four aspects of critical thinking as identifying assumptions, showing that there are various kinds of assumptions; recognising the importance of context, such as general background, historical context, political context and so on; imagining alternatives, which has much in common with creative thinking; and reflective scepticism, which is an habitual reflective stance.

Apostrophe

We use the apostrophe to indicate the missing letter or letters when two words are shortened into one.

e.g. do not = don't (such shortened, informal contractions are not usually used in essays).

It is = it's.

We also use the apostrophe to indicate belonging. This is the possessive apostrophe.

The man's coat is on the hook.

The pupil's coat is on the hook (one pupil).

The pupils' coats are on the hook (more than one pupil).

Words which already have plural forms take the apostrophe before the S as with singular words.

The men's coats are on the hook.

The children's coats are on the hook.

Do not use the apostrophe in the word its when it signifies belonging, rather than a missing letter.

e.g. The stone feels smooth and its surface is warm.

Do not use an apostrophe before an S that is there to indicate a plural, not a possession. This is known as *the greengrocers' apostrophe*

e.g. Orange's – 20p each (incorrect) Oranges – 20p each (correct).

Potatoe's are easy to grow (incorrect) Potatoes are easy to grow (correct).

The 1990's (incorrect) The 1990s (correct).

Appendix 3
Further Reading

Your Recommended Reading List

We have given you the general principles for writing a good essay or assignment, applicable to any of the academic disciplines. For the substance of your essays and assignments, however, you must turn to your recommended reading list. This should contain important and relevant material in your area of study.

General Principles for all Areas of Study

Good English

Greasley, P. (2011) *Doing Essays and Assignments*. London: Sage.
Lucantoni, P. (2014) *Cambridge IGCSE. English as a Second Language. Course Book with Audio CD*. Cambridge: Cambridge University Press.
Osmond, A. (2013) *Academic Writing and Grammar for Students*. London: Sage.
Truss, L. (2003) *Eats, Shoots and Leaves*. London: Fourth Estate.

Critical Thinking

Bowell, T. and Kemp, G. (2002) *Critical Thinking: A Concise Guide* (2nd edition). Abingdon: Routledge.
Brookfield, S.D. (1977) *Developing Critical Thinkers: Challenging Adults to Explore Alternative Ways of Thinking and Acting*. New York: Teachers College Press.
Hospers, J. (1956) *An Introduction to Philosophical Analysis*. London: Routledge.
Mezirow, J. (1981) 'Critical theory of adult learning and education', *Adult Education Quarterly*, 32 (1): 3–24.
Schön, D.H. (1983) *The Reflective Practitioner: How Professionals Think in Action*. New York: Basic Books.

Particular Assignments

Here are some suggestions for further reading about particular kinds of assignments.

Bowden, J. (2011) *Writing a Report* (9th edition). Oxford: How To Books.
Brown, S. and Race, P. (2002) *Lecturing: A Practical Guide*. London: Routledge.
Cottrell, S. (2003) *Skills for Success: The Personal Development Handbook*. Basingstoke: Palgrave Macmillan.
Douglas, T. (2000) *Basic Group Work*. London: Taylor & Francis.

Research Projects

Bell, J. (2005) *Doing Your Research Project: A Guide for First Time Researchers in Education, Health and Social Science* (4th edition). Maidenhead: Open University Press.
Cohen, L., Manion, L. and Morrison, K. (2000) *Research Methods in Education*. London: Routledge.

Appendix 4
Feedback for Chapter Exercises

Exercises for Chapter 1

Practise Three Voices

First Person

In my view the main advantage of books as a source of information is that a book can provide a more comprehensive exploration of a topic than can a journal paper. However, as a student, I have found that articles have the advantage of focus combined with relative brevity. Both books and academic articles in refereed journals will have been scrutinised by independent experts.

Third Person

In the author's view the main advantage of books as a source of information is that a book can provide a more comprehensive exploration of a topic than can a journal paper. However, as a student, the author has found that articles have the advantage of focus combined with relative brevity. Both books and academic articles in refereed journals will have been scrutinised by independent experts.

Passive Voice

It could be argued that the main advantage of books as a source of information is that a book can provide a more comprehensive exploration of the topic than can a journal paper. However, the advantage of the article, for the student, lies in its focus combined with relative brevity. Both books and academic articles in refereed journals will have been scrutinised by independent experts.

A Balanced Use of the Literature

(Too little.) You have not shown knowledge of the literature. You have not shown understanding of the ideas of others.

(Too much.) You have crammed in so much of the work of others that you have not had the space to develop and support your own point of view. You have not shown your ability to be selective in your use of the work of others.

(A balance use.) Your balanced use of the literature demonstrates knowledge and understanding of a manageable number of relevant key thinkers, leaving space to support and develop your own ideas. The number of references bears a sensible relationship to the length of your essay.

Exercise for Chapter 2

Planning Your Essay

Check that your plan has an appropriate introduction to lead into your essay. Perhaps it gives background information or analysis of key terms or simply an outline of the essay to come.

Check that the planned main body of your essay follows a logical sequence. Does it allow scope to reference other writers and to show some criticality and originality?

Check that your plan has an appropriate conclusion to round off your essay.

Exercise for Chapter 3

Argument and Counter Argument

Environmental education should be part of the compulsory curriculum

An argument for this:
The way we treat the environment affects human flourishing and, with global warming, even human survival. Thus environmental knowledge and understanding is so important that it ought to be taught in schools; a part of the compulsory curriculum.

Counter argument:
At the moment there is considerable controversy about environmental matters. For example, many claim that the concern about global warming is mistaken, or at least premature. It would be a mistake to have environmental matters as part of the compulsory curriculum until more facts have been established.

An argument against compulsory environmental education:
The compulsory curriculum is already fully loaded. More cannot be crammed in without detriment to the current compulsory curriculum subjects. Instead the mass media, especially radio and television, could have a role in public understanding about these matters.

Counter argument:
Environmental education is too important not to be part of children's learning in school. However, if time on the timetable is a difficulty, environmental knowledge and understanding could readily permeate other curriculum subjects.

Exercise for Chapter 4

Think About Critical Thinking

Indicative answers to the four questions:

- Thinking which is infected by superstition or by endemic social prejudice is not critical. Wishful thinking is not critical.
- Brookfield's four aspects of critical thinking:

  1. Identifying and challenging assumptions
  2. Recognising the importance of context
  3. Imagining alternatives
  4. Developing a reflective scepticism

- Critical thinking helps us to better understand the material being considered. It generates greater clarity and insight.
- Criticality is important in HE. To write a higher level essay requires demonstrating some critical reflection. Such reflection will increase one's understanding of the essay material, bringing greater clarity and giving greater control of the essay material.

Exercise for Chapter 5

Practise Making Conceptual Distinctions

'Education' and 'Indoctrination'

The concept of education and the concept of indoctrination both apply to human learning, but are very different in all aspects of it: the content of the learning, the process of learning, the intention of the teacher and the outcome for the learner. Whereas 'education' requires that worthwhile learning has taken place, 'indoctrination' can be of false or immoral learning.

The process of education involves an open-ended interaction involving dialogue and respect between teacher and learner. Indoctrination involves rote learning of pre-determined material. The educator's intention is for the learner to achieve understanding and to develop their own point of view. The indoctrinator intends the learner to have unquestioning and unreflective acceptance of the material. Finally, in terms of outcome, the educated learner becomes autonomous, self-directed and critically reflective. The indoctrinated learner, by contrast, becomes closed minded, obedient and uncritical.

'Science' and 'Engineering'

'Science' seeks to understand the nature of the universe, the laws which govern it. 'Engineering' uses that scientific knowledge to create artefacts and systems which work because they conform to the laws of science. For example, aeroplanes would not fly if they were not informed by knowledge of the laws of nature. Scientific thinking is analytic and truth-seeking, whereas engineering thinking is more applied and creative. (This is a relative distinction since scientists can be creative and engineers analytic.)

Meaning

'Category' – A category is a class, a group possessing similar characteristics. To look at the material relevant to your essay and see categories within it demonstrates and develops your understanding of the material. Think how we have divided analysis into four different categories or kinds.

'Metacognition' – Meta means 'beyond' or 'after', and cognition is the actual process of knowing. Metacognition, therefore, means looking beyond the act of knowing, i.e. knowing about knowing! To reflect upon your own acts of knowing is the act of metacognition.

Exercise for Chapter 6

Practise Some Original (Lateral) Thinking

A Brick

A doorstop, to raise a water level, to pin something down, as a weapon, to add weight, to ice and decorate as a cake for a confectioner's shop window display, to mark a spot, to even up a table leg, to throw into a pond to make ripples, to throw into a pond to dislodge a toy boat stuck in leaves.

Original Elements

Original elements could include:

- Developing your own point of view.
- Supporting an established point of view with a new reason.
- Using fresh relevant material – from your professional experience or from a source not on the reading list you have been given.
- Making a plausible link with material outside of your module, for example material in another module.

Exercise for Chapter 7

Practise Cutting Wasted Words

Unpruned Piece

Social workers go into social work because they really want to make a difference to people's lives. They have a desire to work with people and to help them to make their lives better. To be a social worker, a person needs an undergraduate degree in social work or a Master's degree in social work and obviously they must also be properly registered with one of the four recognised UK regulators. They need a wide and extensive range of skills and abilities.

Reduced Piece (reduced by 36 words)

Social workers want to work with people to make a difference to their lives. To be a social worker requires an undergraduate or Master's degree in social work and registration with one of the four recognised UK regulators. Social workers need a wide range of skills.

Exercise for Chapter 8

Two Book Reviews

Helpful reviews assist you to decide if you would like to read the book. They could also be informative in terms of containing some of the book's key facts or ideas and they could be interestingly written. You might gain some useful points for your answer through comparison of the two reviews.

Exercise for Chapter 9

Take a Critical Stance

Next time you listen to a lecture, notice which parts kept your attention. Why? What did you remember later? This kind of critical attention will help you to learn what contributes to a successful lecture. Notice strengths and weaknesses in relation to the lecture's contents and its delivery.

Index

Page numbers in *italics* refer to figures and tables.